Sydney Henry

Order of service

Sydney Henry

Order of service

ISBN/EAN: 9783337126742

Printed in Europe, USA, Canada, Australia, Japan

Cover: Foto ©Andreas Hilbeck / pixelio.de

More available books at **www.hansebooks.com**

ORDER

OF

SERVICE

FOR THE

"KINDERLEHRE"

IN

Evangelical Lutheran Congregations.

———————

COMPILED AND ARRANGED

BY

REV. S. S. HENRY.

———————

NEW HOLLAND, PA.:
GEO. H. RANCK, CLARION OFFICE.
1879.

PREFACE.

This little volume is herewith humbly submitted to the ministers and congregations of the Church for their friendly examination and use. A service of this kind appears to be a felt want in certain localities. It does not propose to establish a *new* order of things, but rather, to restore and employ the *old.* Obedient to the Lord, it would *"stand in the ways, and see, and ask for the old paths, where is the good way, and walk therein."* Jer. 6, 16.

The *Christian instruction of the young, under pastoral supervision,* is a necessity, and a divine command, which must be plain to all the called and ordained teachers in the Church, who solemnly consider the Lord's sacred, standing, injunction to his ministers, *"Feed my lambs."* John 21 : 15.

In some portions of the Church, under existing circumstances, the pastors may not be able to comply with this solemn command of the Lord. Hence, several of our Conferences of the Ger. Ev. Luth. Ministerium of Pennsylvania, have, within recent years, recommended to the pastors to introduce the *Kinderlehre,* leaving the mode of conducting the same to every individual pastor. This would seem to be the only remedy for the cure of a certain deep-rooted evil in the Church. And, in order to be consistent, the name of the service must needs be in harmony with the name of the subject. Where a pastor is not able, on the Lord's day, to give his *personal* attention to this Christian instruction in the congregations of his charge, he may very properly choose some competent person, from among his members, to assist him in this laudable work. To this assistant of the pastor the name *Catechist* is applied in this service. The *office* of Catechist is not new nor unknown in the Christian Church. It has existed at various times and in various parts of the Church, from the days of the early Christian Fathers until the present time. The *Catechist* is to act under the sole direction and supervision of the pastor, and is always amenable to him. His *duty* is, to carry out, as nearly as possible, the order of instruction as previously laid down by the pastor. He is *not* to explain the text of the Catechism, or of the Scripture, but merely to teach or implant the same in the hearts and memories of the children. The same holds good with respect to the other teachers in the *Kinderlehre* who may be called or appointed to assist the Catechist in his work. They are not to teach their own notions and opinions, but simply scriptural texts, if any are assigned, the text in the Catechism, and the Lesson in the Biblical History* appointed for the day by the pastor. The part and duty of teaching or explaining these several texts in the Catechism, etc., belongs properly and officially to the regularly called pastor. A. C. Art. xiv.

The *three Œcumenical Creeds* of the Christian Church are given in their order—with all of which the children of the Church should become familiar. *Luther's Small Catechism* occupies the next place, as to date, in the line of the Church's Confessions. And, as the Church in this year of the Lord, 1879, properly celebrates the 350th anniversary of Luther's master-piece—the Small Catechism—it is but just and fitting that it should be crowned with new honors in every land and clime and be renewedly held up to

---

*The Biblical History, in German and English, published by the *Pilger Book Store, Reading, Pa.*, is herewith heartily recommended.

the Church's children as their goodly heritage, which has come down to them from the Fathers.

The hymns in this service are mostly taken from the *Church Book* and *S. S. Book*. The figures in parentheses ( ) indicate the number of the corresponding hymn in the former. The service has been arranged, partly in view of the number of Sundays in the month, and partly in view of the Five Parts of the Catechism.

May the blessing of God attend this little book on its special mission ; and, wherever it may find an open door of usefulness, may it be of some service in preparing the way for a better order of things, and bring to view, more and more, the Church's important question of the day: *How may we best and most successfully catechize and indoctrinate the children of the Church?*   S. S. H.

HINKLETOWN, *May*, 1879.

TABLE OF CONTENTS.

VI

"Train up a child in the way he should go: and when he is old, he will not depart from it." Prov. xxii : 6.

"And from a child thou hast known the holy Scriptures, which are able to make thee wise unto salvation through faith which is in Christ Jesus." 2 Tim. iii. : 15.

ORDER OF SERVICE.

I. OPENING.

¶ The Pastor or Catechist shall begin the service by saying one of the following sentences, all standing.

THE SENTENCE.

OUR help is in the Name of the Lord: Who made heaven and earth.

THE Lord is high above all people: and His Glory above the heavens.

O GIVE thanks unto the Lord, for He is good: for His mercy endureth for ever.

THIS is the day which the Lord hath made: we will rejoice and be glad in it. We will come before His presence with thanksgiving: and enter into His courts with praise.

HE shall feed His flock like a shepherd: He shall gather the lambs with His arm, and carry them in His bosom.

¶ Then shall the Pastor or Catechist say:

THE VERSICLE.

O Lord, open Thou my lips,

¶ The School shall answer:

And my mouth shall show forth Thy praise.

¶ Then shall be sung a Hymn.

THE HYMN.

¶ *Then shall the Pastor or Catechist and the School say responsively one of the following* Psalms, *at the close of which shall be sung or said the* Gloria Patri.

I. Beatus Vir. Psalm i.

BLESSED is the man that walketh not in the counsel of the ungodly, nor standeth in the way of sinners: nor sitteth in the seat of the scornful.

2. But his delight is in the law of the Lord: and in His law doth he meditate day and night.

3. And he shall be like a tree planted by the rivers of water: that bringeth forth his fruit in his season; his leaf also shall not wither: and whatsoever he doeth shall prosper.

4. The ungodly are not so: but are like the chaff which the wind driveth away.

5. Therefore the ungodly shall not stand in the judgment: nor sinners in the congregation of the righteous.

6. For the Lord knoweth the way of the righteous: but the way of the ungodly shall perish.

Glory be to the Father, and to the Son, and to the Holy Ghost:

As it was in the beginning, is now, and ever shall be, world without end. Amen.

II. Domine, Dominus Noster. Psalm. viii.

O LORD our Lord, how excellent is Thy Name in all the earth: Who hast set Thy Glory above the heavens.

2. Out of the mouth of babes and sucklings hast Thou ordained strength because of Thine enemies: that Thou mightest still the enemy and the avenger.

3. When I consider Thy heavens, the work of Thy fingers: the moon and the stars, which Thou hast ordained;

4. What is man, that Thou art mindful of him?: and the son of man, that Thou visitest him?

5. For Thou hast made him a little lower than the angels: and hast crowned him with glory and honor.

6. Thou madest him to have dominion over the works of Thy hands: Thou hast put all things under his feet.

7. O Lord our Lord: how excellent is Thy Name in all the earth.

Glory be to the Father, etc.

III. Cœli Enarrant. Psalm xix.

THE heavens declare the Glory of God: and the firmament showeth His handy-work.

2. Day unto day uttereth speech: and night unto night showeth knowledge.

3. There is no speech nor language: where their voice is not heard.

4. Their line is gone out through all the earth: and their words to the end of the world.

5. The law of the Lord is perfect, converting the soul: the testimony of the Lord is sure, making wise the simple.

6. The statutes of the Lord are right, rejoicing the heart: the commandment of the Lord is pure, enlightening the eyes.

7. The fear of the Lord is clean, enduring for ever: the judgments of the Lord are true and righteous altogether.

8. More to be desired are they than gold, yea, than much fine gold: sweeter also than honey and the honeycomb.

9. Moreover, by them is Thy servant warned: and in keeping of them there is great reward.

Glory be to the Father, etc.

IV. Dominus Regit Me. Psalm xxiii.

THE Lord is my Shepherd: I shall not want.

2. He maketh me to lie down in green pastures: He leadeth me beside the still waters.

3. He restoreth my soul: He leadeth me in the paths of righteousness for His Name's sake.

4. Yea, though I walk through the valley of the shadow of death, I will fear no evil: for Thou art with me; Thy rod and Thy staff they comfort me.

5. Thou preparest a table before me in the presence of mine enemies: Thou anointest my head with oil; my cup runneth over.

6. Surely goodness and mercy shall follow me all the days of my life: and I will dwell in the house of the Lord for ever.

Glory be to the Father, etc.

V. **Ad Te, Domine.**   Psalm xxv.

UNTO Thee, O Lord, do I lift up my soul: O my God, I trust in Thee.

2. Show me Thy ways, O Lord: teach me Thy paths.

3. Lead me in Thy truth, and teach me: for Thou art the God of my Salvation; on Thee do I wait all the day.

4. Remember, O Lord, Thy tender mercies: and Thy loving-kindness; for they have been ever of old.

5. Remember not the sins of my youth, nor my transgressions: according to Thy mercy remember Thou me for Thy goodness' sake, O Lord.

6. All the paths of the Lord are mercy and truth: unto such as keep His covenant and His testimonies.

Glory be to the Father, etc.

VI. **Benedicam Domino.**   Psalm xxxiv.

I WILL bless the Lord at all times: His praise shall continually be in my mouth.

2. My soul shall make her boast in the Lord: the humble shall hear thereof, and be glad.

3. O magnify the Lord with me: and let us exalt His Name together.

4. The angel of the Lord encampeth round about them that fear Him: and delivereth them.

5. Oh taste and see that the Lord is good: blessed is the man that trusteth in Him.

6. Oh fear the Lord, ye His saints : for there is no want to them that fear Him.

7. Come, ye children, hearken unto me : I will teach you the fear of the Lord.

8. Keep thy tongue from evil : and thy lips from speaking guile.

9. Depart from evil, and do good : seek peace, and pursue it.

10. The eyes of the Lord are upon the righteous : and His ears are open unto their cry.

11. The Lord redeemeth the soul of His servants : and none of them that trust in Him shall be desolate.

Glory be to the Father, etc.

VII. *Lebabi Oculos,* Psalm cxxi.

I WILL lift up mine eyes unto the hills : from whence cometh my help.

2. My help cometh from the Lord : Which made heaven and earth.

3 He will not suffer thy foot to be moved : He that keepeth thee will not slumber.

4. Behold, he that keepeth Israel : shall neither slumber nor sleep.

5. The Lord is thy keeper : the Lord is thy shade upon thy right hand.

6. The sun shall not smite thee by day : nor the moon by night.

7. The Lord shall preserve thee from all evil : He shall preserve thy soul.

8. The Lord shall preserve thy going out and thy coming in : from this time forth, and even for evermore.

Glory be to the Father, etc.

¶ *Then shall be said by the Catechist and School :*

THE TEN COMMANDMENTS.

I AM the Lord thy God : Thou shalt have no other gods before me.

Thou shalt not take the Name of the Lord thy God in vain; for the Lord will not hold him guiltless that taketh his name in vain.

Remember the Sabbath-day to keep it holy.

Honor thy father and thy mother, that thy days may be long upon the land which the Lord thy God giveth thee.

Thou shalt not kill.

Thou shalt not commit adultery.

Thou shalt not steal.

Thou shalt not bear false witness against thy neighbor.

Thou shalt not covet thy neighbor's house.

Thou shalt not covet thy neighbor's wife, nor his man-servant, nor his maid-servant, nor his ox, nor his ass, nor anything that is thy neighbor's.

¶ *Then shall the Catechist say one of the following prayers, or any other suitable prayer. The* Prayer *ended, the School shall sing or say* Amen.

THE PRAYER.

I.

ALMIGHTY and Everlasting God, from Whom cometh every good and perfect gift, send down upon us the healthful spirit of Thy grace. Make those who are called to teach sensible of the great charge which is committed to them. Endue them plenteously with heavenly gifts, and dispose them to rejoice and to labor with diligence in their work. Bless, we humbly beseech Thee, the means which are used to bring up these children in Thy fear and service. May they from the heart believe in Thee, the Lord their God, and worship and serve Thee, the Father, the Son, and the Holy Ghost. Grant them the continual aids of Thy grace, that they may renounce the devil, and all his works, and all his ways, and keep Thy holy will and commandments all the days of their life. Graft in their hearts the love of Thy Name; increase in them true religion; nourish them with all goodness; and of Thy great mercy keep them in the same, that so they may in the end obtain everlasting life; through Jesus Christ, Thy Son, our Lord, Who liveth and reigneth with Thee and the Holy Ghost, ever one God, world without end. *Amen.*

II.

ALMIGHTY and most merciful God, without Whose help we can do nothing that is good, be with us and bless us this day. Bless the instruction which these children shall now receive, and may it by Thy grace be so grafted into their hearts as to bring forth in them the fruits of good living, to the honor and praise of Thy Name. Teach them to believe in Thee, and to love Thee with all their heart, to worship Thee, and to give Thee thanks, to honor Thy Holy Name and Word, and to serve Thee truly all the days of their lives. Bestow Thy blessing upon their instructors, and enable them to teach the truth as it is in Christ Jesus. Be gracious to all who are here before Thee. Pardon our manifold offences, and accept our imperfect prayers. Defend us by day and by night. Build us up in Thy most holy faith. Unite us in the bonds of Christian love. Preserve us from the wickedness that is in the world, and make us a people fearing Thee and working righteousness. These and all things else necessary for us, and for the whole Church, we humbly beg in the Name and for the sake of Jesus Christ our Lord, Who liveth and reigneth with Thee and the Holy Ghost, ever one God, world without end. *Amen.*

III.

O LORD, most loving Saviour and merciful Redeemer, Who didst order little children to come unto Thee, and didst lay Thy hands upon them; look upon us, we humbly beseech Thee, and bless us Thy children, dedicated in holy Baptism to Thy service. Pity the weakness of the tender age of these Thy children, and keep us by Thy grace. Make us to remember our Creator in the days of our youth. Endue us with the fear of God, and make us always mindful of the vow and promise made in our name when we were baptized. Make us dutiful as Thou, O Lord Jesus, wast, unto our parents, loving to our brothers and sisters, obedient to our instructors, respectful to the aged, and meek and gentle to all men; that as we grow in years, we may grow in wisdom and favor with Thee, and with all who are good. Preserve us from all dangers. Let Thy holy Angels be our keepers and defenders, and guide us by Thy

Holy Spirit, that the longer we live the better we may be, to the praise of our school, to the comfort of our parents, to the honor and glory of Thee our Saviour, and to our own happiness here and for ever, O Thou, Who with the Father and the Holy Ghost, livest and reignest ever one God, world without end. *Amen.*

IV.

ALMIGHTY and Everlasting God, Who dost will that not one of these little ones should perish, and hast sent Thine Only Son to seek and to save that which was lost, and through Him hast said, Suffer the little children to come unto me, and forbid them not, for of such is the kingdom of God: Most heartily we beseech Thee so to bless and govern these the children of Thy Church, by Thy Holy Spirit, that they may grow in grace and in the knowledge of Thy Word; protect and defend them against all danger and harm, giving Thy holy Angels charge over them; through Jesus Christ our Lord, Who liveth and reigneth with Thee and the Holy Ghost, ever one God, world without end. *Amen.*

V.

O LORD Jesus Christ, Who, when a child, wast seated in the temple in the midst of the doctors, both hearing them and asking them questions; So rule us, we beseech Thee, by Thy Holy Spirit, that following Thy example, we may love the habitation of Thy house, and the place where Thy honor dwelleth, diligently seek the same, hearing Thy Word with gladness and faithfully keeping it to the saving of our souls, O Thou, Who with the Father and the Holy Ghost, livest and reignest ever one God, world without end. *Amen.*

¶ *Then may be sung or said one of the following* Canticles. *Instead of a* Canticle *a hymn may be sung.*

1. ### Gloria in Excelsis.

GLORY be to God on high;
  And on earth, peace. good will towards men.
We praise Thee, we bless Thee, we worship Thee,
We glorify Thee, we give thanks to Thee for Thy great glory,.

O Lord God, heavenly King,
God the Father Almighty.
O Lord, the only-begotten Son, Jesus Christ;
O Lord God, Lamb of God, Son of the Father,
That takest away the sins of the world, have mercy upon
   us.
Thou that takest away the sins of the world, receive our
   prayer.
Thou that sittest at the right hand of God the Father, have
   mercy upon us.
For Thou only art Holy; Thou only art the Lord.
Thou only, O Christ, with the Holy Ghost, art most high in
   the glory of God the Father. Amen.

2. **Te Deum Laudamus.**

WE praise Thee, O God: we acknowledge Thee to be
   the Lord.
All the earth doth worship Thee: the Father everlasting.
To Thee all angels cry aloud: the heavens, and all the
   powers therein.
To Thee, Cherubim and Seraphim: continually do cry,
Holy, Holy, Holy: Lord God of Sabaoth;
Heaven and earth are full of the Majesty: of Thy Glory.
The glorious company of the Apostles: praise Thee.
The goodly fellowship of the Prophets: praise Thee.
The noble army of Martyrs: praise Thee.
The holy Church throughout all the world: doth acknow-
   ledge Thee;
The Father: of an infinite Majesty;
Thine adorable, true: and only Son;
Also the Holy Ghost: the Comforter.
Thou art the King of Glory: O Christ.
Thou art the everlasting Son: of the Father.
When Thou tookest upon Thee to deliver man: Thou didst
   humble Thyself to be born of a Virgin.
When Thou hadst overcome the sharpness of death: Thou
   didst open the kingdom of heaven to all believers.
Thou sittest at the right hand of God: in the Glory of the
   Father.
We believe that Thou shalt come: to be our Judge.

We therefore pray Thee, help Thy servants: whom Thou
 hast redeemed with Thy precious blood.
Make them to be numbered with Thy saints: in glory ever-
 lasting.
O Lord, save Thy people: and bless Thine heritage.
Govern them: and lift them up for ever.

Day by day: we magnify Thee.
And we worship Thy Name: ever, world without end.
Vouchsafe, O Lord, to keep us this day without sin.
O Lord, have mercy upon us: have mercy upon us.
O Lord, let Thy mercy be upon us: as our trust is in Thee.
O Lord, in Thee have I trusted: let me never be confound-
 ed. *Amen.*

3.   **Magnificat.**

MY soul doth magnify the Lord:
  And my spirit hath rejoiced in God my Saviour.
For He hath regarded:
The low estate of His handmaiden.

For behold, from henceforth:
All generations shall call me blessed.
For He that is mighty hath done to me great things: and
 holy is His Name.
And His mercy is on them that fear Him: from generation
 to generation.

He hath showed strength with His arm:
He hath scattered the proud in the imagination of their
 hearts.
He hath put down the mighty from their seats:
And exalted them of low degree.

He hath filled the hungry with good things:
And the rich He hath sent empty away.
He hath holpen His servant Israel, in remembrance of His
 mercy:
As He spake to our fathers, to Abraham, and to His seed,
 for ever.

4.   **Venite Exultemus Domino.**

OH, come, let us sing unto the Lord:
  Let us make a joyful noise to the Rock of our Salvation.

Let us come before His presence with thanksgiving :
And make a joyful noise unto Him with psalms.
For the Lord is a great God :
And a great King above all gods.
In His hand are the deep places of the earth :
The strength of the hills is His also.
The sea is His, and He made it:
And His hands formed the dry land.
Oh, come, let us worship and bow down :
Let us kneel before the Lord our Maker.
For He is our God:
And we are the people of His pasture, and the sheep of
His hand.
Oh, come, let us sing unto the Lord :
Let us make a joyful noise to the Rock of our Salvation.
Glory be to the Father, and to the Son, and to the Holy
Ghost :
As it was in the beginning, is now, and ever shall be,
world without end. Amen.

5. **Sanctus.**

HOLY, holy, holy, Lord God of Sabaoth :
Heaven and earth are full of Thy glory ;
Hosanna in the highest.
Blessed is He that cometh in the Name of the Lord :
Hosanna in the highest.

¶ *In the service for closing the school may be sung or said,
all standing, the*

6. **Nunc Dimittis.**

LORD, now lettest Thou Thy servant depart in peace :
according to Thy Word ;
For mine eyes have seen Thy salvation : which Thou hast
prepared before the face of all people ;
A light to lighten the Gentiles: and the glory of Thy people Israel.
Glory be to the Father, and to the Son, and to the Holy
Ghost: as it was in the beginning, is now, and ever
shall be, world without end. Amen.

¶ *Then shall the Pastor or Catechist read the* Epistle for the Day.

¶ *Instead of the Epistles and Gospels, the "Scripture Lessons for the Sundays and Festivals of the Church Year," as given in the Church Book on pages* x *and* xi, *may be read, when there is regular service in the church on the same day, in the morning or afternoon.*

¶ *The Catechist shall then say*:

The Epistle (or Scripture Lesson) for [*here he shall name the day*] is written in the—— Chapter of——, beginning at the——Verse.

THE EPISTLE.

¶ The Epistle *ended, he shall say*:

Here endeth the Epistle (or the first Lesson).

¶ *Then shall the* Hallelujah *be sung or said by the School.*

THE HALLELUJAH.

Hallelujah!

¶ *Then, all standing until the end of the Creed, he shall announce the* Gospel for the Day (or the second Lesson), *saying*:

The Holy Gospel is written in the—— Chapter of St.——, beginning at the——Verse.

THE GOSPEL.

¶ The Gospel *ended, he shall say*:

Here endeth the Gospel (or the second Lesson).

¶ *Then all shall say*:

Sanctify us, O Lord, through Thy truth: Thy Word is truth.

¶ *Then shall all unite in saying the* Creed; *either the* Apostles' *or the* Nicene Creed, *may be used.*

THE APOSTLES' CREED.

I BELIEVE in God the Father Almighty, Maker of heaven and earth.

And in Jesus Christ His only Son, our Lord; Who was conceived by the Holy Ghost, Born of the Virgin Mary; Suffered under Pontius Pilate, Was crucified, dead, and buried; He descended into hell; The third day He rose again from the dead; He ascended into heaven, And sitteth on the right hand of God the Father Almighty; From thence He shall come to judge the quick and the dead.

I believe in the Holy Ghost; The holy Christian Church, the Communion of Saints; The Forgiveness of sins; The Resurrection of the body; And the Life everlasting. Amen.

THE NICENE CREED.

I BELIEVE in one God, the Father Almighty, Maker of heaven and earth, And of all things visible and invisible.

And in one Lord Jesus Christ, the Only-begotten Son of God, Begotten of His Father before all worlds, God of God, Light of Light, Very God of very God, Begotten, not made, Being of one substance with the Father, By whom all things were made; Who, for us men, and for our salvation, came down from heaven, And was incarnate by the Holy Ghost of the Virgin Mary, And was made man; And was crucified also for us under Pontius Pilate. He suffered and was buried; And the third day He rose again, according to the Scriptures; And ascended into heaven, And sitteth on the right hand of the Father; And He shall come again with glory to judge both the quick and the dead; Whose kingdom shall have no end.

And I believe in the Holy Ghost, The Lord and Giver of Life, Who proceedeth from the Father and the Son, Who with the Father and the Son together is worshiped and glorified, Who spake by the Prophets. And I believe one holy Christian and Apostolic Church. I acknowledge one Baptism for the remission of sins; And I look for the Resurrection of the dead; And the Life of the world to come. Amen.

II. INSTRUCTION.

¶ *The Catechist shall now follow and carry out the order of Instruction for the day, as previously laid down by the Pastor.*

¶ *If the children are arranged in classes the Catechist may announce the brief lesson in the Catechism, in the Biblical History (and Golden Text), appointed for the day; and the Teachers attend to their duty of teaching the same to the children.*

¶ *The lesson in the Catechism, etc., for the following Sunday, may be announced to the children, to be learned by them during the week, so that, if possible, they may come prepared.*

III. CLOSING.

¶ *The Pastor or Catechist shall now examine the School on the Lesson or Lessons for the day, or on some former Lesson.*

¶ *Announcements shall then be made.*

¶ *Then shall be sung one or more Hymns, or instead of a Hymn, the* Nunc Dimittis, *on page 19, may be sung or said.*

HYMN.

¶ *Then shall the Catechist say one of the following Prayers, at the end of which the School shall say* Amen.

PRAYER.

I.   ON PART FIRST OF THE CATECHISM.

O LORD Jesus Christ, Who wast given both to be a sacrifice for sin, and also an ensample of godly life; Who through Thine obedience hast given an example to all men, especially to the youth and to the children, to render due obedience to their parents and superiors; and, Who didst bid us take up our cross daily and follow Thee; Make, we pray Thee, the yoke of Thy commandments sweet, and the burden of Thy Cross light, unto our souls. Conform us, Thy children, O Father, to the likeness of Thy Blessed Son Jesus Christ. Give us grace that we may strive each day to keep the way of His holy Cross, and carry in our hearts the image of our crucified Master. Thus our lives being formed after His life, may we ever cheerfully and faithfully obey Thy divine will; through Jesus Christ our Lord, Who liveth and reigneth with Thee and the Holy Ghost, ever one God, world without end. *Amen.*

II.   ON PART SECOND OF THE CATECHISM.

ALMIGHTY, Everlasting God, Who hast taught us in the true faith to know and to confess that Thou, God the Father, Son, and Holy Ghost, art one eternal God full of grace and compassion; Who hast created, redeemed and sanctified us according to Thine infinite love and mercy; we beseech Thee that Thou wouldest at all times keep us steadfast in this faith and grant us grace, that we may always honor, praise and glorify Thee, Who livest and reignest, ever one God, world without end. *Amen.*

III.   ON PART THIRD OF THE CATECHISM.

LORD God, our heavenly Father, Who, through Jesus Christ, Thy dear Son, hast taught us, that we shall call upon Thee with all cheerfulness and confidence, even as beloved children entreat their affectionate parent: we beseech Thee that Thou wouldest at all times graciously accept and answer our prayer and supplication, to the end that we may evermore praise and thank Thee : through the same Thy dear Son, our Lord, Who liveth and reigneth with Thee and the Holy Ghost, ever one God, world without end. *Amen.*

IV.   ON PART FOURTH OF THE CATECHISM.

ALMIGHTY and most merciful · God, our heavenly Father, we give Thee thanks that in the Sacrament of Holy Baptism, Thou hast received us as Thy children, and granted us for Christ's sake, forgiveness of sin and everlasting life; So rule us, we beseech Thee, by Thy Holy Spirit, that we may never be unmindful of our baptismal covenant, but daily renounce every evil way, and serve Thee in true holiness, until we come at last into Thy heavenly kingdom ; through Jesus Christ our Lord, Who liveth and reigneth with Thee and the Holy Ghost, ever one God, world without end. *Amen.*

MOST merciful God, our heavenly Father, we give Thee hearty thanks, that through Jesus Christ Thy dear Son, Thou hast instituted for us the Holy Supper of our Lord, in which under the consecrated Bread and Wine He gives us to eat and to drink His true Body and Blood for the forgiveness of our sins; and we beseech Thee, grant us grace, that in Thine own good time, we may be found ready to be admitted to the same, may worthily receive these Thy precious Gifts and be strengthened thereby to walk in holiness of life, until we come at last to endless joy, through the same Thy dear Son, our Lord Jesus Christ, Who liveth and reigneth with Thee and the Holy Ghost, ever one God, world without end. *Amen.*

¶ *Then shall all unite in saying*

THE LORD'S PRAYER.

OUR Father, Who art in heaven; Hallowed be Thy Name; Thy kingdom come; Thy will be done on earth, as it is in heaven; Give us this day our daily bread; And forgive us our trespasses, as we forgive those who trespass against us; And lead us not into temptation; But deliver us from evil; For Thine is the kingdom, and the power, and the glory, for ever and ever. Amen.

¶ *Then shall be sung*

THE DOXOLOGY.

¶ *When the Doxology is ended, a few moments may be spent in silent prayer, after which all may depart quietly and in order. The following prayer may be used.*

SILENT PRAYER.

Create in me a clean heart, O God; and renew a right spirit within me. Cast me not away from Thy presence; and take not Thy Holy Spirit from me. Restore unto me the joy of Thy salvation; and uphold me with Thy free Spirit. Amen.

SYMBOLUM QUICUNQUE.

(ATHANASIAN CREED.)

WHOSOEVER will be saved: before all things it is necessary that he hold the Christian Faith.

2. Which Faith except every one do keep whole and undefiled: without doubt he shall perish everlastingly.

3. And the Christian Faith is this: That we worship one God in Trinity, and Trinity in Unity;

4. Neither confounding the Persons: nor dividing the Substance.

5. For there is one Person of the Father, another of the Son: and another of the Holy Ghost.

6. But the Godhead of the Father, of the Son, and of the Holy Ghost, is all one: the Glory equal, the Majesty co-eternal.

7. Such as the Father is, such is the Son: and such is the Holy Ghost.

8. The Father uncreate, the Son uncreate: and the Holy Ghost uncreate.

9. The Father incomprehensible, the Son incomprehensible: and the Holy Ghost incomprehensible.

10. The Father eternal, the Son eternal: and the Holy Ghost eternal.

11. And yet there are not three eternals: but one eternal.

12. As also there are not three incomprehensibles, nor three uncreated: but one uncreated, and one incomprehensible.

13. So likewise the Father is Almighty, the Son Almighty: and the Holy Ghost Almighty.

14. And yet there are not three Almighties: but one Almighty.

15. So the Father is God, the Son is God: and the Holy Ghost is God.

16. And yet there are not three Gods: but one God.

17. So likewise the Father is Lord, the Son Lord: and the Holy Ghost Lord.

18. And yet not three Lords: but one Lord.

19. For like as we are compelled by the Christian verity: to acknowledge every Person by himself to be God and Lord;

20. So are we forbidden by the Christian Religion: to say, There be three Gods, or three Lords.

21. The Father is made of none: neither created, nor begotten.

22. The Son is of the Father alone: not made, nor created, but begotten.

23. The Holy Ghost is of the Father and of the Son: neither made, nor created, nor begotten, but proceeding.

24. So there is one Father, not three Fathers: one Son, not three Sons: one Holy Ghost, not three Holy Ghosts.

25. And in this Trinity none is afore, or after other: none is greater, or less than another;

26. But the whole three Persons are co-eternal together: and co-equal.

27. So that in all things: as is aforesaid: the Unity in Trinity, and the Trinity in Unity is to be worshipped.

28. He therefore that will be saved: must thus think of the Trinity.

29. Furthermore, it is necessary to everlasting salvation: that he also believe rightly the Incarnation of our Lord Jesus Christ.

30. For the right Faith is, that we believe and confess: that our Lord Jesus Christ, the Son of God, is God and Man.

31. God, of the substance of the Father, begotten before the worlds: and Man, of the Substance of his Mother, born in the world;

32. Perfect God and perfect Man: of a reasonable soul and human flesh subsisting;

33. Equal to the Father, as touching his Godhead; and inferior to the Father, as touching his Manhood.

34. Who although he be God and Man: yet he is not two, but one Christ;

35. One; not by conversion of the Godhead into flesh; but by taking of the Manhood into God;

36. One altogether; not by confusion of Substance: but by Unity of Person.

37. For as the reasonable soul and flesh is one man: so God and Man is one Christ;

38. Who suffered for our salvation: descended into hell, rose again the third day from the dead.

39. He ascended into heaven, he sitteth on the right hand of the Father, God Almighty: from whence he shall come to judge the quick and the dead.

40. At whose coming all men shall rise again with their bodies; and shall give account for their own works.

41. And they that have done good shall go into life everlasting; and they that have done evil into everlasting fire.

42. This is the Christian Faith: which except a man believe faithfully, he cannot be saved.

LUTHER'S SMALL CATECHISM.

PART I.

THE TEN COMMANDMENTS.

In the plain form in which they are to be taught by the Head of a family.

THE FIRST COMMANDMENT.

I am the Lord thy God. Thou shalt have no other gods before me.

[Thou shalt not make unto thee any graven image. or any likeness of anything that is in heaven above, or that is in the earth beneath, or that is in the water under the earth; thou shalt not bow down thyself to them, nor serve them: for I the Lord thy God am a jealous God, visiting the iniquity of the fathers upon the children unto the third and fourth generation of them that hate me; and showing mercy unto thousands of them that love me, and keep my commandments.]

What is meant by this Commandment?

Answer. We should fear, love, and trust in God above all things.

THE SECOND COMMANDMENT.

Thou shalt not take the name of the Lord thy God in vain; for the Lord will not hold him guiltless that taketh his name in vain.

What is meant by this Commandment?

Answer. We should so fear and love God as not to curse, swear, conjure, lie, or deceive, by his name, but call upon him in every time of need, and worship him with prayer, praise, and thanksgiving.

28

THE THIRD COMMANDMENT.

Remember the sabbath day, to keep it holy.

[Six days shalt thou labor, and do all thy work ; but the seventh day is the sabbath of the Lord thy God : in it thou shalt not do any work, thou, nor thy son, nor thy daughter, nor thy manservant, nor thy maidservant, nor thy cattle, nor thy stranger that is within thy gates : for in six days the Lord made heaven and earth, the sea, and all that in them is, and rested the seventh day : wherefore the Lord blessed the sabbath day, and hallowed it.]

What is meant by this Commandment?

Answer. We should so fear and love God as not to despise his word and the preaching of the gospel, but deem it holy, and willingly hear and learn it.

THE FOURTH COMMANDMENT.

Honor thy father and thy mother, that thy days may be long upon the land which the Lord thy God giveth thee.

What is meant by this Commandment?

Answer. We should so fear and love God, as not to despise nor displease our parents and superiors, but honor, serve, obey, love, and esteem them.

THE FIFTH COMMANDMENT.

Thou shalt not kill.

What is meant by this Commandment?

Answer. We should so fear and love God, as not to do our neighbor any bodily harm or injury, but rather assist and comfort him in danger and want.

THE SIXTH COMMANDMENT.

Thou shalt not commit adultery.

What is meant by this Commandment?

Answer. We should so fear and love God, as to be chaste and pure in our words and deeds, each one also loving and honoring his wife or her husband.

THE SEVENTH COMMANDMENT.

Thou shalt not steal.

What is meant by this Commandment?

Answer. We should so fear and love God, as not to rob our neighbor of his money or property, nor bring it into our possession by unfair dealing or fraudulent means, but rather assist him to improve and protect it.

THE EIGHTH COMMANDMENT.

Thou shalt not bear false witness against thy neighbor.

What is meant by this Commandment?

Answer. We should so fear and love God as not deceitfully to belie, betray, slander, nor raise injurious reports against our neighbor, but apologize for him, speak well of him, and put the most charitable construction on all his actions.

THE NINTH COMMANDMENT.

Thou shalt not covet thy neighbor's house.

What is meant by this Commandment?

Answer. We should so fear and love God, as not to desire by craftiness to gain possession of our neighbor's inheritance or home, or to obtain it under the pretext of a legal right, but be ready to assist and serve him in the preservation of his own.

THE TENTH COMMANDMENT.

Thou shalt not covet thy neighbor's wife, nor his manservant, nor his maidservant, nor his ox, nor his ass, nor anything that is thy neighbor's.

What is meant by this Commandment?

Answer. We should so fear and love God as not to alienate our neighbor's wife from him, entice away his servants, nor let loose his cattle, but use our endeavors that they may remain and discharge their duty to him.

What does God declare concerning all these Commandments?

Answer. He says: I the Lord thy God am a jealous God, visiting the iniquity of the fathers upon the children unto the third and fourth generation of them that hate me: and showing mercy unto thousands of them that love me, and keep my commandments.

What is meant by this declaration?

Answer. God threatens to punish all those who transgress these commandments. We should, therefore, dread his displeasure, and not act contrarily to these commandments. But he promises grace and every blessing to all who keep them. We should, therefore, love and trust in him, and cheerfully do what he has commanded us.

PART II.

THE CREED.
In the plain form in which it is to be taught by the Head of a family.

THE FIRST ARTICLE.
Of Creation.

I believe in God the Father Almighty, Maker of heaven and earth.

What is meant by this Article?

Answer. I believe that God has created me and all that exists; that he has given and still preserves to me my body and soul with all my limbs and senses, my reason and all the faculties of my mind, together with my raiment, food, home, and family, and all my property; that he daily provides me abundantly with all the necessaries of life, protects me from all danger, and preserves me and guards me against all evil; all which he does out of pure, paternal, and divine goodness and mercy, without any merit or worthiness in me; for all which I am in duty bound to thank, praise, serve, and obey him. This is most certainly true.

THE SECOND ARTICLE.
Of Redemption.

And in Jesus Christ His only Son, our Lord; who was conceived by the Holy Ghost, born of the Virgin Mary; suffered under Pontius Pilate, was crucified, dead, and buried; He descended into hell; the third day he rose again from the dead; He ascended into heaven, and sitteth on the right hand of God the Father Almighty; from thence He shall come to judge the quick and the dead.

What is meant by this Article?

Answer. I believe that Jesus Christ, true God, begotten of the Father from eternity, and also true man, born of the Virgin Mary, is my Lord ; who has redeemed me, a lost and condemned creature, secured and delivered me from all sins, from death, and from the power of the devil, not with silver and gold, but with his holy and precious blood, and with his innocent sufferings and death ; in order that I might be his, live under him in his kingdom, and serve him in everlasting righteousness, innocence and blessedness ; even as he is risen from the dead, and lives and reigns to all eternity. This is most certainly true.

THE THIRD ARTICLE.

Of Sanctification.

I believe in the Holy Ghost ; the holy Christian Church, the Communion of Saints ; the Forgiveness of sins ; the Resurrection of the body ; and the Life everlasting. Amen.

What is meant by this Article?

Answer. I believe that I cannot by my own reason or strength believe in Jesus Christ my Lord, or come to him ; but the Holy Ghost has called me through the gospel, enlightened me by his gifts, and sanctified and preserved me in the true faith : in like manner as he calls, gathers, enlightens, and sanctifies the whole Christian Church on earth, and preserves it in union with Jesus Christ in the true faith : in which Christian Church he daily forgives abundantly all my sins, and the sins of all believers, and will raise up me and all the dead at the last day, and will grant everlasting life to me and to all who believe in Christ. This is most certainly true.

PART III.

THE LORD'S PRAYER.

In the plain form in which it is to be taught by the
Head of a family.

THE INTRODUCTION.

Our Father who art in heaven.

What is meant by this Introduction ?

Answer. God would thereby affectionately encourage us to believe that he is truly our Father, and that we are his children indeed, so that we may call upon him with all cheerfulness and confidence, even as beloved children entreat their affectionate parent.

THE FIRST PETITION.

Hallowed be thy name.

What is meant by this Petition ?

Answer. The name of God is indeed holy in itself; but we pray in this petition that it may be hallowed also by us.

How is this effected ?

Answer. When the word of God is taught in its truth and purity, and we, as the children of God, lead holy lives, in accordance with it; to this may our blessed Father in heaven help us! But whoever teaches and lives otherwise than as God's word prescribes, profanes the name of God among us; from this preserve us, Heavenly Father!

THE SECOND PETITION.

Thy kingdom come.

What is meant by this Petition ?

Answer. The kingdom of God comes indeed of itself, without our prayer; but we pray in this petition that it may come unto us also.

When is this effected ?

Answer. When our heavenly Father gives us his Holy Spirit, so that by his grace we believe his holy word, and live a godly life here on earth, and in heaven for ever.

THE THIRD PETITION.

Thy will be done on earth, as it is in heaven.

What is meant by this Petition ?

Answer. The good and gracious will of God is done indeed without our prayer; but we pray in this petition that it may be done by us also.

When is this effected ?

Answer. When God frustrates and brings to nought every evil counsel and purpose, which would hinder us from hallowing the name of God, and prevent his kingdom from coming to us, such as the will of the devil, of the world, and of our own flesh; and when he strengthens us, and keeps us steadfast in his word and in the faith, even unto our end. This is his gracious and good will.

THE FOURTH PETITION.

Give us this day our daily bread.

What is meant by this Petition ?

Answer. God gives indeed without our prayer even to the wicked also their daily bread; but we pray in this petition that he would make us sensible of his benefits, and enable us to receive our daily bread with thanksgiving.

What is implied in the words: "our daily bread ?"

Answer. All things that pertain to the wants and the support of this present life; such as food, raiment, money, goods, house and land, and other property; a believing spouse and good children; trustworthy servants and faithful magistrates; favorable seasons, peace and health; education and honor; true friends, good neighbors, and the like.

THE FIFTH PETITION.

And forgive us our trespasses, as we forgive those who trespass against us.

What is meant by this Petition ?

Answer. We pray in this petition, that our heavenly Father would not regard our sins, nor deny us our requests on account of them; for we are not worthy of anything for which we pray, and have not merited it; but that he would grant us all things through grace, although we daily commit much sin, and deserve chastisement alone. We will therefore, on our part, both heartily forgive, and also readily do good to those who may injure or offend us.

THE SIXTH PETITION.

And lead us not into temptation.

What is meant by this Petition?

Answer. God indeed tempts no one to sin; but we pray in this petition that God would so guard and preserve us, that the devil, the world, and our own flesh, may not deceive us, nor lead us into error and unbelief, despair, and other great and shameful sins; and that, though we may be thus tempted, we may nevertheless finally prevail and gain the victory.

THE SEVENTH PETITION.

But deliver us from evil.

What is meant by this Petition?

Answer. We pray in this petition, as in a summary, that our heavenly Father would deliver us from all manner of evil, whether it affect the body or soul, property or character, and, at last, when the hour of death shall arrive, grant us a happy end, and graciously take us from this world of sorrow to himself in heaven.

THE CONCLUSION.

For thine is the kingdom, and the power, and the glory, for ever and ever. Amen.

What is meant by the word "Amen"?

Answer. That I should be assured that such petitions are acceptable to our heavenly Father, and are heard by him; for he himself has commanded us to pray in this manner, and has promised that he will hear us. Amen, Amen, that is, Yea, yea, it shall be so.

PART IV.

THE SACRAMENT OF HOLY BAPTISM.

In the plain form in which it is to be taught by the Head of a family.

I. *What is Baptism?*

Answer. Baptism is not simply water, but it is the water comprehended in God's command, and connected with God's word.

What is that word of God?

Answer. It is that which our Lord Jesus Christ spake, as it is recorded in the last chapter of Matthew, verse 19:

"Go ye, and teach all nations, baptizing them in the name of the Father, and of the Son, and of the Holy Ghost."

II. *What gifts or benefits does Baptism confer?*

Answer. It worketh forgiveness of sins, delivers from death and the devil, and confers everlasting salvation on all who believe, as the word and promise of God declare.

What are such words and promises of God?

Answer. Those which our Lord Jesus Christ spake, as they are recorded in the last chapter of Mark, verse 16: "He that believeth and is baptized, shall be saved; but he that believeth not, shall be damned."

III. *How can water produce such great effects?*

Answer. It is not the water indeed that produces these effects, but the word of God which accompanies and is connected with the water, and our faith, which relies on the word of God connected with the water. For the water, without the word of God, is simply water and no baptism. But when connected with the word of God, it is a baptism, that is, a gracious water of life and a "washing of regeneration" in the Holy Ghost; as St. Paul says to Titus, in the third chapter, ver. 5–8: "According to his mercy he saved us, by the washing of regeneration, and renewing of the Holy Ghost; which he shed on us abundantly through Jesus Christ our Saviour; that being justified by his grace, we should be made heirs according to the hope of eternal life. This is a faithful saying."

IV. *What does such baptizing with water signify?*

Answer. It signifies that the old Adam in us is to be drowned and destroyed by daily sorrow and repentance, together with all sins and evil lusts; and that again the new man should daily come forth and rise, that shall live in the presence of God in righteousness and purity for ever.

Where is it so written?

Answer. St. Paul, in the Epistle to the Romans, chapter 6, verse 4, says: "We are buried with Christ by baptism into death; that like as he was raised up from the dead by the glory of the Father, even so we also should walk in newness of life."

OF CONFESSION.

What is Confession?

Answer. Confession consists of two parts: the one is, that we confess our sins; the other, that we receive absolution or forgiveness through the pastor as of God himself, in no wise doubting, but firmly believing that our sins are thus forgiven before God in heaven.

What sins ought we to confess?

Answer. In the presence of God we should acknowledge ourselves guilty of all manner of sins, even of those which we do not ourselves perceive; as we do in the Lord's Prayer. But in the presence of the pastor we should confess those sins alone, of which we have knowledge, and which we feel in our hearts.

Which are these?

Answer. Here reflect on your condition, according to the Ten Commandments, namely: Whether you are a father or mother, a son or daughter, a master or mistress, a manservant or maidservant—whether you have been disobedient, unfaithful, slothful—whether you have injured any one by words or actions—whether you have stolen, neglected, or wasted aught, or done other evil.

PART V.

THE SACRAMENT OF THE ALTAR,

OR,

THE LORD'S SUPPER.

In the plain form in which it is to be taught by the Head of a family.

What is the Sacrament of the Altar?

Answer. It is the true body and blood of our Lord Jesus Christ, under the bread and wine, given unto us Christians to eat and to drink, as it was instituted by Christ himself.

Where is it so written?

Answer. The holy Evangelists, Matthew, Mark, and Luke, together with St. Paul, write thus:

"Our Lord Jesus Christ, the same night in which he was betrayed, took bread: and when he had given thanks, he brake it, and gave it to the disciples, and said, Take, eat; this is my body, which is given for you: this do, in remembrance of me.

"After the same manner also he took the cup, when he had supped, gave thanks, and gave it to them, saying, Drink ye all of it: this cup is the new testament in my blood, which is shed for you, for the remission of sins: this do ye, as oft as ye drink it, in remembrance of me."

What benefits are derived from such eating and drinking?

Answer. They are pointed out in these words: "given, and shed for you, for the remission of sins." Namely, through these words, the remission of sins, life and salvation are granted unto us in the Sacrament. For where there is remission of sins, there are also life and salvation.

How can the bodily eating and drinking produce such great effects?

Answer. The eating and the drinking, indeed, do not produce them, but the words which stand here, namely: "given, and shed for you, for the remission of sins." These words are, besides the bodily eating and drinking, the chief things in the Sacrament: and he who believes these words, has that which they declare and set forth, namely, the remission of sins.

Who is it, then, that receives this Sacrament worthily?

Answer. Fasting and bodily preparation are indeed a good external discipline; but he is truly worthy and well prepared, who believes these words: "given, and shed for you, for the remission of sins." But he who does not believe these words, or who doubts, is unworthy and unfit; for the words: "FOR YOU," require truly believing hearts.

MORNING AND EVENING PRAYER.
AND PRAYER BEFORE AND AFTER MEAT.

In the form in which they are to be taught by the Head of a family.

¶ [*The following Order of Morning and Evening* Prayer *may also be used as an Order of Family Prayer, the Head of the family saying the opening Sentence, and the closing* Prayer, *and all the members together saying the* Apostles' Creed *and the* Lord's Prayer. *A Hymn may be sung before the* Creed.]

MORNING PRAYER.

¶ *In the Morning, when thou risest, thou shalt say:*

In the Name of the Father, and of the Son, and of the Holy Ghost. Amen.

¶ *Then, kneeling or standing, thou shalt say the* Apostles' Creed *and the* Lord's Prayer, *as here followeth:*

THE APOSTLES' CREED.

I believe in God the Father Almighty, Maker of heaven and earth.

And in Jesus Christ His only Son, our Lord; Who was conceived by the Holy Ghost, Born of the Virgin Mary; Suffered under Pontius Pilate, Was crucified, dead, and buried; He descended into hell; The third day He rose again from the dead; He ascended into heaven. And sitteth on the right hand of God the Father Almighty; From thence He shall come to judge the quick and the dead.

I believe in the Holy Ghost; The holy Christian Church, the communion of saints; The Forgiveness of sins; The Resurrection of the body; And the Life everlasting. Amen.

THE LORD'S PRAYER.

Our Father who art in Heaven; Hallowed be Thy name; Thy kingdom come; Thy will be done on earth, as it is in heaven; Give us this day our daily bread; And forgive us our trespasses, as we forgive those who trespass against us; And lead us not into temptation; But deliver us from evil;

For Thine is the kingdom, and the power, and the glory, for ever and ever. Amen.

¶ *Then shalt thou say this Prayer :*

I Give thanks unto Thee, Heavenly Father, through Jesus Christ Thy dear Son, that Thou hast protected me through the night from all danger and harm; and I beseech Thee to preserve and keep me, this day also, from all sin and evil; that in all my thoughts, words, and deeds, I may serve and please Thee. Into Thy hands I commend my body and soul, and all that is mine. Let Thy holy angel have charge concerning me, that the wicked one have no power over me. *Amen.*

EVENING PRAYER.

¶ *In the Evening, when thou goest to bed, thou shalt say :*

In the Name of the Father, and of the Son, and of the Holy Ghost. Amen.

¶ *Then, kneeling or standing, thou shalt say the* Apostles' Creed *and the* Lord's Prayer.

¶ *Then shalt thou say this Prayer :*

I Give thanks unto Thee, Heavenly Father, through Jesus Christ Thy dear Son, that Thou hast this day so graciously protected me, and I beseech Thee to forgive me all my sins, and the wrong which I have done, and by Thy great mercy defend me from all the perils and dangers of this night. Into Thy hands I commend my body and soul, and all that is mine. Let Thy holy angel have charge concerning me, that the wicked one have no power over me. *Amen.*

GRACE BEFORE MEAT.

¶ *Before meat, the members of the family standing at the table reverently and with folded hands, there shall be said :*

The eyes of all wait upon Thee, O Lord: and Thou givest them their meat in due season. Thou openest Thine hand, and satisfiest the desire of every living thing.

¶ *Then shall be said the* Lord's Prayer, *and after that this* Prayer:

O LORD God, Heavenly Father, bless unto us these Thy gifts, which of Thy tender kindness Thou hast bestowed upon us, through Jesus Christ our Lord. Amen.

THANKS AFTER MEAT.

¶ *After meat, all standing reverently and with folded hands, there shall be said:*

O GIVE thanks unto the Lord, for He is good: for His mercy endureth for ever. He giveth food to all flesh: He giveth to the beast his food, and to the young ravens which cry. The Lord taketh pleasure in them that fear Him: in those that hope in His mercy.

¶ *Then shall be said the* Lord's Prayer, *and after that this* Prayer:

WE give thanks to Thee, O God our Father, for all Thy benefits, through Jesus Christ our Lord, Who with Thee liveth and reigneth, for ever and ever. Amen.

TABLE OF DUTIES.

Or, certain passages of the Scriptures, selected for various orders and conditions of men, wherein their respective duties are set forth.

BISHOPS, PASTORS, AND PREACHERS.

A bishop must be blameless, the husband of one wife, vigilant, sober, of good behavior, given to hospitality, apt to teach; not given to wine, no striker, not greedy of filthy lucre; but patient, not a brawler, not covetous; one that ruleth well his own house, having his children in subjection with all gravity: not a novice, but holding fast the faithful word as he hath been taught, that he may be able by sound doctrine both to exhort and to convince the gainsayers. 1 *Tim.* 3 : 2-6 : *Tit.* 1 :9.

HEARERS.

"For the laborer is worthy of his hire." *Luke* 10 : 7.

"Even so hath the Lord ordained, that they which preach the gospel should live of the gospel." 1 *Cor.* 9 : 14.

C

"Let him that is taught in the word, communicate unto him that teacheth, in all good things; Be not deceived; God is not mocked: for whatsoever a man soweth, that shall he also reap." *Gal.* 6 : 6, 7.

"Let the elders that rule well, be counted worthy of double honor, especially they who labor in the word and doctrine ; For the Scripture saith, Thou shalt not muzzle the ox that treadeth out the corn : And, The laborer is worthy of his reward." 1 *Tim.* 5 : 17, 18.

"And we beseech you, brethren, to know them which labor among you ; and are over you in the Lord and admon-. ish you ; And to esteem them very highly in love for their work's sake. And be at peace among yourselves." 1 *Thess.* 5 : 12, 13.

"Obey them that have the rule over you, and submit yourselves: for they watch for your souls, as they that must give account, that they may do it with joy. and not with grief: for that is unprofitable for you." *Heb.* 13 : 17.

MAGISTRATES.

Let every soul be subject unto the higher powers. For there is no power but of God: the powers that be are ordained of God; for rulers are not a terror to good works, but to the evil. Wilt thou then not be afraid of the power? do that which is good, and thou shalt have praise of the same; for he is the minister of God to thee for good. But if thou do that which is evil, be afraid; for he beareth not the sword in vain: for he is the minister of God, a revenger to exe-cute wrath upon him that doeth evil. *Rom.* 13 : 1–4.

HUSBANDS.

Ye husbands, dwell with your wives according to know-ledge, giving honor unto the wife, as unto the weaker ves-sel, and as being heirs together of the grace of life; that your prayers be not hindered. 1 *Pet.* 3 : 7. And be not bitter against them. *Col.* 3 : 10.

WIVES.

Wives, submit yourselves unto your husbands, as unto the Lord.—Even as Sarah obeyed Abraham, calling him lord: whose daughters ye are, as long as ye do well, and are not afraid with any amazement. *Eph.* 5 : 22; 1 *Pet.* 3 : 6.

PARENTS.

Ye fathers, provoke not your children to wrath: but bring them up in the nurture and admonition of the Lord. *Eph.* 6:4.

CHILDREN.

Children, obey your parents in the Lord: for this is right. Honor thy father and mother; which is the first commandment with promise; that it may be well with thee, and thou mayest live long on the earth. *Eph.* 6:1-3.

MALE AND FEMALE SERVANTS, AND LABORERS.

Servants, be obedient to them that are your masters according to the flesh, with fear and trembling, in singleness of your heart, as unto Christ; not with eyeservice, as men-pleasers; but as the servants of Christ, doing the will of God from the heart; with good will doing service, as to the Lord, and not to men; knowing that whatsoever good thing any man doeth, the same shall he receive of the Lord, whether he be bond or free. *Eph.* 6:5-8.

MASTERS AND MISTRESSES.

Ye masters, do the same things unto them, forbearing threatening: knowing that your Master also is in heaven; neither is there respect of persons with him. *Eph.* 6:9.

YOUNG PERSONS, IN GENERAL.

Likewise, ye younger, submit yourselves unto the elder. Yea, all of you be subject one to another, and be clothed with humility: for God resisteth the proud, and giveth grace to the humble. Humble yourselves therefore under the mighty hand of God, that he may exalt you in due time. 1 *Pet.* 5:5, 6.

WIDOWS.

She that is a widow indeed, and desolate, trusteth in God, and continueth in supplications and prayers night and day; but she that liveth in pleasure is dead while she liveth. I *Tim.* 5:5, 6.

CHRISTIANS, IN GENERAL.

Thou shalt love thy neighbor as thyself. Herein are comprehended all the commandments. *Rom.* 13 : 9, 10.   And persevere in prayer for all men.   1 *Tim.* 2 : 1, 2.

𝕷et eac𝔥 one learn 𝔥is lesson well,
𝕿𝔥en peace s𝔥all in our 𝔥ouse𝔥olds dwell.

CHRISTIAN QUESTIONS AND ANSWERS.

¶ *After Confession and Instruction in the Ten Commandments, Creed, Lord's Prayer, and the Holy Sacraments,
the pastor, or each one for himself, may ask the following
questions:*

1. *Do you believe that you are a sinner?*

Yes, I believe it; I am a sinner.

2. *How did you obtain the knowledge thereof?*

From the holy decalogue or commandments; these I have not kept.

3. *Do you feel sorrow on account of your sins?*

Yes, I feel sorrow for having sinned against God.

4. *What have you deserved of God on account of your sins?*

His wrath and displeasure, temporal death and eternal damnation.   Rom. 6 : 21, 23.

5. *But do you still hope to be saved?*

Yes, such is my hope.

6. *Whence do you derive this hope and comfort?*

From my blessed Lord and Saviour Jesus Christ.

7. *Who is Christ?*

The Son of God, true God and man.

8. *Are there more Gods than one?*

No, there is one God only, but there are three persons, Father, Son, and Holy Ghost.

9. *What has Christ done for you that you find comfort in him?*

He died for me, shedding his blood on the cross for me, for the forgiveness of my sins. Gal. 2 : 20. 2 Tim. 4: 6-8.

10. *Did the Father also die for you?*

He did not: for the Father is God only, and the Holy Ghost is also God only; but the Son is true God and true man, who died for me, shedding his blood for me.

11. *How do you obtain this knowledge?*

From the holy Gospel, and from the words of the Sacrament; and also from his body and blood in the Sacrament, which are given to me as a pledge. 2 Cor. 1 : 22.—5 : 5. Eph. 1 : 13, 14.

12. *What are these words?*

"Our Lord Jesus Christ, the same night in which he was betrayed, took bread: and when he had given thanks, he brake it, and gave it to the disciples, and said, Take, eat; this is my body, which is given for you: this do, in remembrance of me. After the same manner also he took the cup, when he had supped, gave thanks, and gave it to them, saying, Drink ye all of it: this cup is the new testament in my blood, which is shed for you, for the remission of sins: this do ye, as oft as ye drink it, in remembrance of me."

13. *Do you then believe that the true body and blood of Christ are in the Sacrament?*

Yes, this I believe.

14. *What induces you to believe it?*

The words of Christ: "Take, eat; this is my body: drink ye all of it; this is my blood."

15. *What are we to do when we partake of his body and blood, and thus receive the pledge?*

We should show his death (1 Cor. 11 : 26) and the shedding of his blood, and also remember that which he taught us: "This do, as oft as ye do it, in remembrance of me."

16. *Why should we remember and show his death?*

That we might learn to believe that no creature was able to make satisfaction for our sins; but that Christ, true God and man, alone was able: further, that we might learn to tremble on account of our sins, to regard them as very great, and to rejoice and find comfort in Christ alone; and that thus we might, through this faith, be saved.

17. *What was it that moved him to die for your sins and make atonement for them?*

His great love to his Father, and also to me and other sinners, as it is written in John 14 : 31; Rom. 5 : 11; Gal. 2 : 20; Eph. 5 : 2, 25.

18. *But why do you desire to receive the Sacrament?*

In order that I might learn to believe that Christ died for my sins, through his great love, as now stated; and then, that I might learn from him to love God and my neighbor.

19. *What should admonish and incite a Christian to receive the Sacrament of the Altar frequently?*

On the part of God, he should be so moved both by the command of the Lord Jesus Christ ["do this"], and also by his promise ["given and shed for you for the remission of sins"]. In reference to himself, he should be so moved by his own spiritual burdens which oppress him, on account of which, indeed, such commandment, encouragement and promise are given.

20. *But what shall such persons do, who do not feel these burdens, or who do not hunger or thirst for the Sacrament?*

To these no better counsel can be given than, *First*, to examine whether they are not still flesh and blood, and by all means to believe all that the Scriptures say of these things in Gal. 5 : 16–21, and in Rom. 7 : 18.

Secondly, they should reflect whether they do not still dwell in an evil world, and also remember that sins and dangers are continually found therein, as the Scriptures declare in John 15: 18–20.—16: 7–11; 1 John 2: 15–17.—5:4, 5.

Thirdly, they should consider that they are exposed to the snare of Satan, who continually (1 Pet. 5 : 8) disturbs their inward and outward peace by falsehood and deadly delusions, according to the representations of the Scriptures in John 8 : 44.—16 : 32; 1 Pet. 5 : 8, 9; 2 Tim. 2 : 26; Eph. 6 : 11–16.

HYMNS.

1 (1)   L. M.

BEFORE Jehovah's awful throne,
  Ye nations, bow with sacred joy:
Know that the Lord is God alone,
He can create, and He destroy.

2 His sovereign power, without our aid,
  Made us of clay, and formed us men;
And when like wandering sheep we strayed,
He brought us to His fold again.

3 We are His people, we His care,
  Our souls and all our mortal frame;
What lasting honors shall we rear,
Almighty Maker, to Thy Name?

4 We'll crowd Thy gates with thankful songs,
  High as the heavens our voices raise;
And earth, with her ten thousand tongues,
Shall fill Thy courts with sounding praise.

5 Wide as the world is Thy command,
  Vast as eternity Thy love;
Firm as a rock Thy truth must stand,
When rolling years shall cease to move.

2   *Lobe den Herren, den Mœchtigen Kœnig.*   14.14.4.7.8.

PRAISE thou the Lord, the omnipotent King of creation,
  This, O my soul, is my earnest, devout aspiration.
    Join in the throng!
    Psalter and harp aid in song!
  High sound the hymn of laudation.

2 Praise thou the Lord, who controlleth all ever so surely,
Who, as on wings of an eagle, hath borne thee securely.
Who doth thee keep,
Whether awake or asleep,
Hast thou not felt this so truly?

3 Praise thou the Lord, who so fearfully, wondrously made
thee,
Who lent thee health and thy strength, and so graciously
How oft in need   [led thee.
Hath God so kindly indeed
Spread wings of mercy around thee!

4 Praise thou the Lord, thy estate He so visibly tending,
Streams of love down from the heavens on thee has been
Think of it, man,   [sending.
What the Omnipotent can,
Who is with love to thee bending.

5 Praise thou the Lord, O my soul, all within me bless His
Name,
All that breathe, praise ye with Abraham's children the
He is thy Light,   [self-same.
Soul, keep it ever in sight,
Praising Him, end thou with Amen.

3 (14) *   8. 7.

MIGHTY God, while angels bless Thee,
May a mortal lisp Thy Name?
Lord of men as well as angels,
Thou art every creature's theme.

2 Lord of every land and nation,
Ancient of eternal days!
Sounded through the wide creation
Be Thy just and lawful praise.

3 For the grandeur of Thy nature,
Grand beyond a seraph's thought;
For created works of power,
Works with skill and kindness wrought.

*Verse 4 in Ch. B. omitted.

4 But Thy rich, Thy free Redemption,
Dark through brightness all along—
Thought is poor, and poor expression:
Who dare sing that awful song!

5 From the highest throne in glory
To the Cross of deepest woe!
All to ransom guilty captives!
Flow, my praise, forever flow.

4 (3) *Psalm 95.* S. M

COME, sound His praise abroad,
And hymns of glory sing!
Jehovah is the sovereign God,
The universal King.

2 He formed the deeps unknown:
He gave the seas their bound:
The watery worlds are all His own,
And all the solid ground.

3 Come, worship at His throne:
Come, bow before the Lord:
We are His works and not our own.
He formed us by His word.

4 To-day attend His voice,
Nor dare provoke His rod:
Come, like the people of His choice,
And own your gracious God!

5 (73) * *Psalm 103.* S. M.

O BLESS the Lord, my soul!
Let all within me join,
And aid my tongue to bless His Name,
Whose favors are divine.

2 O bless the Lord, my soul!
Nor let His mercies lie
Forgotten in unthankfulness.
And without praises die.

*Verse 5 om.

3 'Tis He forgives thy sins;
  'Tis He relieves thy pain;
  'Tis He that heals thy sicknesses,
  And gives thee strength again.

4 He crowns thy life with Love,
  When ransomed from the grave;
  He that redeemed my soul from death
  Hath sovereign power to save.

5 His wondrous works and ways
  He made by Moses known;
  But sent the world His truth and grace
  By His beloved Son.

6 (20)   *Alleluia, dulce carmen.*

ALLELUIA! best and sweetest
    Of the hymns of praise above!
Alleluia! thou repeatest,
  Angel host, these notes of love.
      This ye utter,
  While your golden harps ye move.

2 Alleluia! Church victorious,
  Join the concert of the sky!
  Alleluia! bright and glorious,
    Lift, ye saints, this strain on high!
      We, poor exiles,
    Join not yet your melody.

3 Alleluia! strains of gladness
    Suit not souls with anguish torn:
  Alleluia! sounds of sadness
    Best become our state forlorn;
      Our offences
    We with bitter tears must mourn.

4 But our earnest supplication,
    Holy God, we raise to Thee:
  Visit us with Thy salvation,
    Make us all Thy joys to see!
      Alleluia!
    Ours at length this strain shall be.

7   *For Infant Classes.*   8. 7. D.

HUMBLE praises, holy Jesus,
    Infant voices raise to Thee:
In Thy mercy, O receive us!
    Suffer us Thy lambs to be.
Chorus.—Halleluia, sweetly singing,
    Joyful tribute now we bring.
Halleluia, Halleluia!
    Halleluia, to our King.

2 Gracious Saviour, be Thou with us;
    Let Thy mercy richly flow:
Give Thy Spirit, blessed Jesus!
    Light and life on us bestow.
Chorus.—Halleluia, sweetly singing, etc.

8   (215) *   C. M.

ALL hail the power of Jesus' Name!
    Let angels prostrate fall ;
Bring forth the royal diadem,
    And crown Him Lord of all.

2 Hail Him, ye heirs of David's line,
    Whom David Lord did call;
The God incarnate, Man divine :
    And crown Him Lord of all.

3 Let every kindred, every tribe,
    On this terrestrial ball,
To Him all majesty ascribe,
    And crown Him Lord of all.

4 O that with yonder sacred throng
    We at His feet may fall;
We'll join the everlasting song,
    And crown Him Lord of all.

9   (11)   *Nun danket alle Gott.*   6.7.6.7.6.6.6.6.

NOW thank we all our God,
    With heart and hands and voices,

---

*Verses 2 and 4 om.

Who wondrous things hath done,
In whom His earth rejoices;
Who from our mother's arms
Hath blessed us on our way
With countless gifts of love,
And still is ours to day.

2 O may this bounteous God,
Through all our life be near us,
With ever joyful hearts,
And blessed peace to cheer us;
And keep us in His grace,
And guide us when perplexed,
And free us from all ills,
In this world and the next.

3 All praise and thanks to God
The Father, now be given,
The Son and Him Who reigns
With them in highest heaven;
The One eternal God,
Whom earth and heaven adore;
For thus it was, is now,
And shall be evermore!

10   *Schœnster Herr Jesu.*   5.5.7.5.5.8.

BEAUTIFUL Saviour! King of creation!
Son of God and Son of man!
Truly I'd love Thee, Truly I'd serve Thee,
Light of my soul, my Joy, my Crown.

2 Fair are the meadows, Fairer the woodlands,
Robed in flowers of blooming Spring;
Jesus is fairer, Jesus is purer;
He makes our sorrowing spirit sing.

3 Fair is the sunshine, Fairer the moonlight
And the sparkling stars on high;
Jesus shines brighter, Jesus shines purer,
Than all the angels in the sky.

4 Beautiful Saviour! Lord of the nations!
  Son of God and Son of man!
Glory and honor,   Praise, adoration,
  Now and for evermore be Thine!

11 (12)   7s.

HOLY, holy, holy Lord!
  Be Thy glorious Name adored.
Lord, Thy mercies never fail:
Hail, celestial Goodness, hail!

2 Though unworthy, Lord, Thine ear
  Deign our humble songs to hear.
Purer praise we hope to bring,
When around Thy throne we sing.

3 There no tongue shall silent be;
  All shall join in harmony;
That through heaven's capacious round
Praise to Thee may ever sound.

4 Lord, Thy mercies never fail:
  Hail, celestial Goodness, hail!
Holy, holy, holy Lord!
Be Thy glorious Name adored.

OPENING HYMNS.

12   8. 7.

IN Thy Name, O Lord, assembling,
  We Thy children now draw near;
Teach us to rejoice with trembling:
  Speak, and let Thy servants hear,—
    Hear with meekness,—
  Hear Thy Word with godly fear.

2 While our days on earth are lengthened,
  Help us give them, Lord, to Thee;
In Thy service hourly strengthened,
  May we never weary be.
    Till Thy glory
  In the world of light we see.

3 Then in worship purer, sweeter,
  Thee Thy children will adore,
Tasting joys far higher, greater
  Than were e'er conceived before,
    Praising, serving,
  Thee, our God, for evermore.

13 (22)   *Zeige Dich uns ohne Huelle.*   7s.

LORD, remove the veil away,
  Let us see Thyself to-day!
Thou who camest from on high,
For our sins to bleed and die,
Help us now to cast aside
All that would our hearts divide;
With the Father and the Son
Let Thy living Church be one.

2 O, from earthly cares set free,
  Let us find our rest in Thee!
May our cares and conflicts cease
In the calm of Sabbath peace,
That Thy people here below
Something of the bliss may know,
Something of the rest and love
In the Sabbath home above!

3 Lord, Thy sinful child prepare
For a place and portion there!
Give my soul the spotless dress
Of Thy perfect Righteousness:
Then at length, a welcome guest,
I shall enter to the feast,
Earthly cares and sorrows o'er,
Joys to last for evermore.

14 (35)   C. M.

BLEST day of God, most calm, most bright,
  The first and best of days;
The laborer's rest, the saint's delight,
  The day of prayer and praise!

2 My Saviour's face made thee to shine,
　His rising did thee raise;
This made thee heavenly and divine
　Beyond the common days.

3 The first fruits oft a blessing prove
　To all the sheaves behind;
And they that do a Sabbath love,
　A happy week shall find.

4 This day must I 'fore God appear,
　For, Lord, the day is Thine;
O let me spend it in Thy fear,
　Then shall the day be mine.

15　　　　　　　　　　　　　　　　　　L. M.

ASSEMBLED in our school once more,
　　O Lord, Thy blessing we implore;
We meet to read, and sing, and pray;
Be with us then through this Thy day.

2 Our fervent prayer to Thee ascends,
For parents, teachers, foes, and friends;
And when we in Thy house appear,
Help us to worship in Thy fear.

3 When we on earth shall meet no more,
May we above to glory soar;
And praise Thee in more lofty strains,
Where one eternal Sabbath reigns.

16 (37)　　　　　　　　　　　　　　　　7s.

SAFELY through another week,
　God has brought us on our way:
Let us now a blessing seek,
　Waiting in His courts to-day;
Day of all the week the best,
Emblem of eternal rest.

2 Mercies multiplied each hour
　Through the week, our praise demand;
Guarded by Thy mighty power,
　Fed and guided by Thy hand;

Though ungrateful we have been.
Only made returns of sin.

3 While we pray for pardoning grace,
   Through the dear Redeemer's name,
Show Thy reconciling face,
   Take away our sin and shame:
From our worldly cares set free,
May we rest this day in Thee.

4 Here we're come, Thy Name to praise;
   Let us feel Thy presence near:
May Thy glory meet our eyes,
   While we in Thy house appear:
Here afford us, Lord, a taste
Of our everlasting feast.

5 May the Gospel's joyful sound
   Conquer sinners, comfort saints;
Make the fruits of grace abound,
   Bring relief for all complaints.
Thus may all our Sabbaths prove,
Till we join the Church above.

17 (49) *Herr Jesu Christ, Dich zu uns wend.* L. M.

LORD Jesus Christ, be present now!
   And let Thy Holy Spirit bow
All hearts in love and fear to-day,
To hear the truth and keep Thy way.

2 Open our lips to sing Thy praise,
Our hearts in true devotion raise,
Strengthen our faith, increase our light,
That we may know Thy Name aright:

3 Until we join the host that cry
"Holy art Thou, O Lord most High!"
And 'mid the light of that blest place
Shall gaze upon Thee face to face.

4 Glory to God, the Father, Son,
And Holy Spirit, Three in One!
To Thee, O blessed Trinity.
Be praise throughout eternity!

18 (526)   C. 4.

SHEPHERD of tender youth,
Guiding in love and truth
Through devious ways:
Christ, our triumphant King,
We come Thy Name to sing,
And here our children bring.
To join Thy praise.

2 Thou art our holy Lord,
O all-subduing Word,
Healer of strife:
Thou didst Thyself abase,
That from sin's deep disgrace
Thou mightest save our race,
And give us life.

3 O wisdom's great High Priest!
Thou hast prepared the feast
Of holy love;
And in our mortal pain
None calls on Thee in vain;
Help Thou dost not disdain,
Help from above.

4 Ever be near our side,
Our Shepherd and our Guide,
Our staff and song:
Jesus, Thou Christ of God,
By Thine enduring Word,
Lead us where Thou hast trod;
Make our faith strong.

5 So now, and till we die.
Sound we Thy praises high,
And joyful sing:
Let all the holy throng
Who to Thy Church belong,
Unite and swell the song
To Christ our King!

D

CLOSING HYMNS.

19 (58)   8. 7.

L ORD, dismiss us with Thy blessing,
   Fill our hearts with joy and peace!
Let us each, Thy Love possessing,
   Triumph in redeeming grace.
     O refresh us,
   Travelling through this wilderness.

2 Thanks we give and adoration
   For Thy Gospel's joyful sound.
May the fruits of Thy salvation
   In our hearts and lives abound:
     May Thy presence
   With us evermore be found.

3 So, whene'er the signal's given
   Us from earth to call away,
Borne on angels' wings to heaven,
   Glad the summons to obey,
     May we, ready,
   Rise and reign in endless day.

20 (57)   H. M.

O N what has now been sown,
   Thy blessing, Lord, bestow;
The power is Thine alone
   To make it spring and grow:
Do Thou the gracious harvest raise,
And Thou alone shalt have the praise.

2 To Thee our wants are known,
   From Thee are all our powers,
Accept what is Thine own,
   And pardon what is ours:
Our praises, Lord, and prayers receive,
And to Thy Word a blessing give.

3 O grant that each of us,
   Who meet before Thee here,

May meet together thus,
When Thou and Thine appear,
And follow Thee to heaven our home;
Even so, Amen, Lord Jesus, come!

21 (59) *Ach bleib mit Deiner Gnade.* 7. 6.

ABIDE with us, our Saviour,
Nor let Thy mercy cease;
From Satan's might defend us,
And grant our souls release.

2 Abide with us, our Saviour,
Sustain us by Thy Word;
That we with all Thy people
To life may be restored.

3 Abide with us, our Saviour,
Thou Light of endless light;
Increase to us Thy blessings,
And save us by Thy might.

4 To Father, Son, and Spirit,
Eternal One and Three,
As was, and is for ever,
All praise and glory be.

22 8. 7.

HEAVENLY Father, send Thy blessing
On Thy children gathered here,
May they all, Thy Name confessing,
Be to Thee for ever dear.

2 May they be like Joseph, loving,
Dutiful, and chaste, and pure;
And their faith, like David, proving,
Steadfast unto death endure.

3 Holy Saviour, Who in meekness
Didst vouchsafe a child to be,
Guide their steps and help their weakness,
Bless and make them like to Thee.

4 Spread Thy golden pinions o'er them,
Holy Spirit, from above;

Guide them, lead them, go before them,
 Give them peace, and joy, and love.

5 Temples of the Holy Spirit,
 May they with Thy glory shine,
And immortal bliss inherit,
 And for evermore be Thine.

———

MORNING.

23 (510)   L. M.

A WAKE, my soul, and with the sun
 Thy daily stage of duty run;
Shake off dull sloth, and joyful rise
To pay thy morning sacrifice.

2 Wake and lift up thyself, my heart,
 And with the angels bear thy part,
Who all night long unwearied sing
High praise to the eternal King.

3 All praise to Thee, who safe hast kept,
 And hast refreshed me while I slept:
Grant, Lord, when I from death shall wake,
I may of endless life partake!

4 Lord, I my vows to Thee renew;
 Disperse my sins as morning dew;
Guard my first springs of thought and will,
And with Thyself my spirit fill.

5 Direct, control, suggest, this day,
 All I design, or do, or say;
That all my powers, with all their might,
In Thy sole glory may unite.

6 Praise God, from whom all blessings flow;
 Praise Him, all creatures here below;
Praise Him, above, ye heavenly host,
Praise Father, Son, and Holy Ghost.

24 (512) *Jam Lucis orto Sidere.* C. M.

NOW that the sun is beaming bright,
    Once more to God we pray,
That He, the uncreated Light,
    May guide our souls this day.

2 No sinful word, no deed of wrong,
    Nor thoughts that idly rove;
But simple truth be on our tongue,
    And in our hearts be love.

3 And while the hours in order flow,
    O Christ, securely fence
Our gates beleaguered by the foe,
    The gate of every sense.

4 And grant that to Thine honor, Lord,
    Our daily toil may tend:
That we begin it at Thy word,
    And in Thy favor end.

EVENING.

25 (522) L. M.

ALL praise to Thee, my God, this night,
    For all the blessings of the light:
Keep me, O keep me, King of kings,
Beneath Thine own Almighty wings! .

2 Forgive me, Lord, for Thy dear Son,
The ill that I this day have done:
That with the world, myself, and Thee,
I, ere I sleep, at peace may be.

3 Teach me to live, that I may dread
The grave as little as my bed;
To die, that this vile body may
Rise glorious at the awful day.

4 O when shall I, in endless day,
For ever chase dark sleep away,
And hymns divine with angels sing
In endless praise to Thee, my King?

5 Praise God, from whom all blessings flow;
 Praise Him, all creatures here below;
 Praise Him, above, ye heavenly host;
 Praise Father, Son, and Holy Ghost.

26 (517)   10s.

A BIDE with me! fast falls the eventide;
 The darkness deepens: Lord, with me abide!
When other helpers fail, and comforts flee,
Help of the helpless, O abide with me!

2 Swift to its close ebbs out life's little day;
 Earth's joys grow dim, its glories pass away;
 Change and decay in all around I see;
 O Thou who changest not, abide with me!

3 Not a brief glance I beg, a passing word,
 But as Thou dwell'st with Thy disciples, Lord,
 Familiar, condescending, patient, free,
 Come, not to sojourn, but abide with me!

4 Come not in terrors as the King of kings,
 Be kind and good, with healing on Thy wings;
 Tears for all woes, a heart for every plea;
 O Friend of sinners, thus abide with me!

5 Thou on my head in early youth didst smile,
 And, though rebellious and perverse meanwhile,
 Thou hast not left me oft as I left Thee:
 On to the close, O Lord, abide with me!

6 I need Thy presence every passing hour:
 What but Thy grace can foil the tempter's power?
 Who like Thyself my guide and stay can be?
 Through cloud and sunshine, O abide with me!

27 (523)   L. M.

S UN of my soul, Thou Saviour dear,
 It is not night if Thou be near;
O may no earth-born cloud arise
To hide Thee from Thy servant's eyes.

2 When the soft dews of kindly sleep
My wearied eyelids gently steep,
Be my last thought, how sweet to rest
For ever on my Saviour's breast.

3 Abide with me from morn till eve,
For without Thee I cannot live,
Abide with me when night is nigh,
For without Thee I dare not die.

4 If some poor wandering child of Thine
Has spurned to-day the voice divine,
Now, Lord, the gracious work begin;
Let him no more lie down in sin.

5 Watch by the sick; enrich the poor
With blessings from Thy boundless store;
Be every mourner's sleep to-night,
Like infant's slumbers, pure and light.

6 Come near and bless us when we wake,
Ere through the world our way we take;
Till in the ocean of Thy love
We lose ourselves in Heaven above.

THE CHURCH YEAR.
ADVENT.

28 (126)   8. 7.

COME, Thou long-expected Jesus,
   Born to set Thy people free;
From our fears and sins release us,
   Let us find our rest in Thee.
Israel's Strength and Consolation,
   Hope of all the earth Thou art;
Dear Desire of every nation,
   Joy of every longing heart.

2 Born Thy people to deliver;
   Born a child, yet God our King:
Born to reign in us for ever,
   Now Thy gracious kingdom bring.

By Thine own eternal Spirit,
　　Rule in all our hearts alone;
By Thine all-sufficient merit,
　　Raise us to Thy glorious throne.

29　(111)　　　*Jordanis oras prævia.*　　　L. M.

ON Jordan's banks the Herald's cry
　　Announces that the Lord is nigh:
Come then and hearken, for he brings
Glad tidings from the King of kings.

2 Then cleansed be every breast from sin,
　Make straight the way for God within,
　And let us all our hearts prepare
　For Christ to come and enter there.

3 For Thou art our Salvation, Lord,
　Our Refuge and our great Reward.
　Without Thy grace our life must fade,
　And wither like a flower decayed.

4 Stretch forth Thy hand, to health restore,
　And make us rise to fall no more:
　Once more upon Thy people shine,
　And fill the world with love divine.

5 To Him who left the throne of heaven
　To save mankind, all praise be given:
　Like praise be to the Father done,
　And Holy Spirit Three in One.

30　(123)　　　　　　　　　　　C. M.

HARK, the glad sound, the Saviour comes,
　　The Saviour promised long!
Let every heart prepare a throne,
　　And every voice a song.

2 On Him the Spirit. largely poured,
　　Exerts His sacred fire;
　Wisdom and might, and zeal and love,
　　His holy breast inspire.

3 He comes the prisoner to release,
In Satan's bondage held:
The gates of brass before Him burst,
The iron fetters yield.

4 He comes from thickest films of vice
To clear the mental ray,
And on the eyeballs of the blind
To pour celestial day.

5 He comes the broken heart to bind,
The bleeding soul to cure,
And with the treasures of His grace
To enrich the humble poor.

6 Our glad hosannas, Prince of Peace!
Thy welcome shall proclaim;
And heaven's eternal arches ring
With Thy beloved Name.

31 (113)　　*En clara vox redarguit.*　　8. 7.

HARK! an awful voice is sounding:
"Christ is nigh!" it seems to say;
"Cast away the dreams of darkness,
O ye children of the day!"

2 Startled at the solemn warning,
Let the earth-bound soul arise;
Christ, her Sun, all sloth dispelling,
Shines upon the morning skies.

3 Lo, the Lamb, so long expected,
Comes with pardon down from heaven,
Let us haste, with tears of sorrow,
One and all, to be forgiven.

4 So, when next He comes with glory,
Wrapping all the earth in fear,
With His mercy He may shield us,
And with words of love draw near.

32 (114) *   *Wie soll ich Dich empfangen?*

O HOW shall I receive Thee,
　　How greet Thee, Lord, aright?
All nations long to see Thee,
　　My hope, my heart's delight!
O kindle, Lord, most holy,
　　Thy lamp within my breast,
To do in spirit lowly
　　All that may please Thee best.

2 Thy Zion palms is strewing,
　　And branches fresh and fair;
My heart, its powers renewing,
　　An anthem shall prepare.
My soul puts off her sadness
　　Thy glories to proclaim;
With all her strength and gladness
　　She fain would serve Thy Name.

3 Love caused Thy Incarnation,
　　Love brought Thee down to me.
Thy thirst for my salvation
　　Procured my liberty.
O Love beyond all telling,
　　That led Thee to embrace,
In love all love excelling,
　　Our lost and fallen race!

4 Rejoice then, ye sad-hearted,
　　Who sit in deepest gloom,
Who mourn o'er joys departed,
　　And tremble at your doom:
He who alone can cheer you,
　　Is standing at the door;
He brings His pity near you,
　　And bids you weep no more.

---

*Verse 3 in Ch. B. om.

33 (116) * *Ermuntert euch, ihr Frommen.*　　7. 6.

REJOICE, all ye believers,
　And let your lights appear!
The evening is advancing,
　And darker night is near.
The Bridegroom is arising,
　And soon He draweth nigh.
Up! pray, and watch, and wrestle;
　At midnight comes the cry!

2. The watchers on the mountain
　Proclaim the Bridegroom near;
Go meet Him as He cometh,
　With hallelujahs clear.
The marriage-feast is waiting,
　The gates wide-open stand;
Up, up, ye heirs of glory;
　The Bridegroom is at hand!

3 Our Hope and Expectation,
　O Jesus, now appear;
Arise, Thou Sun so longed for,
　O'er this benighted sphere!
With hearts and hands uplifted,
　We plead, O Lord, to see
The day of earth's redemption,
　That brings us unto Thee!

CHRISTMAS.

34 (127)　　　　　　　　　　　　8. 7.

HARK! what mean those holy voices
　Sweetly sounding through the skies?
Lo! the angelic host rejoices;
　Heavenly hallelujahs rise.

2 Listen to the wondrous story,
　Which they chant in hymns of joy:

---

*Verse 3 in Ch. B. om.

"Glory in the highest, glory!
  Glory be to God most high!

3 "Peace on earth, good-will from heaven,
  Reaching far as man is found;
Souls redeemed, and sins forgiven;
  Loud our golden harps shall sound.

4 "Christ is born, the great Anointed;
  Heaven and earth His praises sing!
O receive whom God appointed
  For your Prophet, Priest, and King.

5 "Hasten, mortals, to adore Him;
  Learn His Name, and taste His joy;
Till in heaven ye sing before Him,
  Glory be to God most high!"

6 Let us learn the wondrous story
  Of our great Redeemer's birth;
Spread the brightness of His glory,
  Till it cover all the earth.

35 (128)   7s.

HARK! the herald-angels sing,
  "Glory to the new-born King;
Peace on earth, and mercy mild,
God and sinners reconciled!"

2 Joyful, all ye nations, rise,
  Join the triumph of the skies;
Universal nature say,
Christ the Lord is born to-day!

3 Christ, by highest heaven adored,
  Christ, the everlasting Lord:
Late in time behold Him come,
Offspring of a virgin's womb!

4 Veiled in flesh, the Godhead see,
  Hail the incarnate Deity!
Pleased as man with men to appear,
Jesus, our Immanuel here!

5 Hail, the heavenly Prince of Peace,
  Hail, the Sun of Righteousness!
  Light and life to all He brings,
  Risen with healing in His wings.

6 Mild He lays His glory by,
  Born that man no more may die;
  Born to raise the sons of earth;
  Born to give them second birth.

7 Come, Desire of nations, come,
  Fix in us Thy humble home;
  O, to all Thyself impart,
  Formed in each believing heart!

36   *Stille Nacht, heilige Nacht!*   6.6.8.9.6.

SILENT night! Holy night!
  All is calm, all is bright,
Round yon Virgin Mother and Child!
Holy Infant, so tender and mild,
  Sleep in heavenly peace.

2 Silent night! Holy night!
  Shepherds quake at the sight!
  Glories stream from Heaven afar,
  Heavenly hosts sing Alleluia,
    Christ, the Saviour, is born!

3 Silent night! Holy night!
  Son of God, love's pure light
  Radiant beams from Thy holy Face,
  With the dawn of redeeming grace,
    Jesus, Lord, at Thy birth.

37   C. M.

HOSANNA! Raise the pealing hymn
  To David's Son and Lord;
With cherubim and seraphim
  Exalt the incarnate Word.

2 Hosanna! Lord, our feeble tongue
  No lofty strains can raise:

But Thou wilt not despise the young,
    Who meekly chant Thy praise.

3 Hosanna! Master, lo! we bring
    Our offerings to Thy throne;
Not gold, nor myrrh, nor mortal thing,
    But *hearts* to be Thine own.

4 Hosanna! Once Thy gracious ear
    Approved a lisping throng:
Be gracious still, and deign to hear
    Our poor but grateful song.

5 O Saviour, if, redeemed by Thee,
    Thy Temple we behold,
Hosannas, through eternity,
    We'll sing to harps of gold!

38 (131)   *Vom Himmel hoch da komm ich her.*   **L. M.**

GOOD news from heaven the angels bring,
    Glad tidings to the earth they sing:
To us this day a Child is given,
To crown us with the joy of heaven.

2 This is the Christ, our God and Lord,
Who in all need shall aid afford;
He will Himself our Saviour be,
From all our sins to set us free.

3 To us that blessedness He brings,
Which from the Father's bounty springs:
That in the heavenly realm we may
With Him enjoy eternal day.

4 All hail, Thou noble Guest, this morn,
Whose Love did not the sinner scorn:
In my distress Thou comest to me;
What thanks shall I return to Thee?

5 Were earth a thousand times as fair,
Beset with gold and jewels rare,
She yet were far too poor to be
A narrow cradle, Lord, for Thee.

6 Ah, dearest Jesus, holy Child,
Make Thee a bed, soft, undefiled,
Within my heart, that it may be
A quiet chamber kept for Thee.

7 Praise God upon His heavenly throne,
Who gave to us His only Son:
For this His hosts, on joyful wing,
A blest New Year of mercy sing.

39 *Det kimer nu til Julefest.* L. M.

THE happy Christmas comes once more,
The heavenly Guest is at the door,
The blessed words the shepherds thrill,
The joyous tidings: Peace, Good-will.

2 To David's city let us fly,
Where angels sing beneath the sky;
Through plain and village pressing near,
And news from God with shepherds hear.

3 O let us go with quiet mind,
The gentle Babe with shepherds find,
To gaze on Him who gladdens them,
The loveliest flower of Jesse's stem.

4 The lowly Saviour meekly lies,
Laid off the splendor of the skies;
No crown bedecks His forehead fair,
No pearl, nor gem, nor silk is there.

5 No human glory, might and gold,
The lovely Infant's form enfold;
The manger and the swaddlings poor
Are His, whom angels' songs adore.

6 O wake our hearts, in gladness sing,
And keep our Christmas with our King,
Till living song, from loving souls,
Like sound of mighty waters rolls.

7 O holy Child, Thy manger streams
Till earth and heaven glow with its beams,

Till midnight noon's bright light has won,
And Jacob's Star outshines the sun.

8 Thou Patriarch's joy, Thou Prophet's song,
Thou heavenly Day-Spring, looked for long,
Thou Son of man, Incarnate Word,
Great David's Son, great David's Lord!

9 Come, Jesus, glorious heavenly Guest,
Keep Thine own Christmas in our breast,
Then David's harp-strings, hushed so long,
Shall swell our Jubilee of song.

40 (132)   *Freut euch, ihr lieben Christen.*   7. 6.

REJOICE, rejoice, ye Christians,
  With all your hearts, this morn!
O hear the blessed tidings,
  "The Lord, the Christ, is born!"
Now brought us by the angels
  That stand about God's throne;
O lovely are the voices
  That make such tidings known!

2 O hearken to their singing!
  This Child shall be your Friend;
The Father so hath willed it.
  That thus your woes should end.
The Son is freely given,
  That in Him ye may have
The Father's grace and blessing,
  And know He loves to save.

3 Nor deem the form too lowly
  That clothes Him at this hour;
For know ye what it hideth?
  'Tis God's almighty power.
Though now within the manger
  So poor and weak He lies,
He is the Lord of all things,
  He reigns above the skies.

4 Sin, death, and hell, and Satan
  Have lost the victory;
This Child shall overthrow them,
  As ye shall surely see.
Their wrath shall naught avail them;
  Fear not, their reign is o'er;
This Child shall overthrow them;
  O hear, and doubt no more!

41 (104)   C. M.

JOY to the world! the Lord is come!
    Let earth receive her King:
Let every heart prepare Him room,
  And heaven and nature sing.

2 Joy to the earth! the Saviour reigns!
  Let men their songs employ;
While fields and floods, rocks, hills, and plains
  Repeat the sounding joy.

3 No more let sins and sorrows grow,   .
  Nor thorns infest the ground;
He comes to make His blessings flow
  Far as the curse is found.

4 He rules the world with truth and grace,
  And makes the nations prove
The glories of His righteousness,
  And wonders of His love.

42 (129)   *Adeste Fideles.*   11s.

COME hither, ye faithful, triumphantly sing:
    Come see in the manger the angels' dread King!
To Bethlehem hasten, with joyful accord;
O come ye, come hither, to worship the Lord!

2 True Son of the Father, He comes from the skies;
To be born of a Virgin, He does not despise:
To Bethlehem hasten, with joyful accord;
O come ye, come hither, to worship the Lord!

E

3 Hark, hark to the angels, all singing in heaven,
"To God in the highest all glory be given!"
To Bethlehem hasten, with joyful accord;
O come ye, come hither, to worship the Lord!

4 To Thee, then, O Jesus, this day of Thy birth,
Be glory and honor through heaven and earth.
True Godhead incarnate, omnipotent Word!
O come, let us hasten to worship the Lord!

43   *Infants' Christmas Carol.*   7.7.7.4.7.

CHRIST was born on Christmas Day,
    Wreathe the holly, twine the bay,
Christ the Lord is born to-day,
    The Babe, the Son,
    The Holy Child of Mary.

2 He is born to set us free,
He is born our Lord to be,
Carol, carol joyfully:
    The Babe, the Son, etc.

3 Let the bright red berries glow,
Everywhere in goodly show,
Christ the Lord is come, you know,
    The Babe, the Son, etc.

4 Christian men rejoice and sing;
'T is the birthday of our King,
Every one your anthem bring,
    To God, the Lord.
    The Holy Child of Mary.

44   8. 7.

NOW we bring our Christmas treasures,
    Loving thoughts and deeds we bring,
Childlike hearts we gladly offer
    To the Child, the children's King.
To the Child, who, in the manger,
    Lay upon that Christmas morn,
When the angels came to tell us
    That the children's King was born.

2 And He lives, throughout the ages,—
  Lives and reigns in earth and sky;
Angel hosts still sing the glory
  Of the children's King on high.
Yet He cares for children's praises:
  So, with heart and voice we ring;
Glory in the highest, glory
  To the Child, the children's King!"

THE NAME OF JESUS.

45 (223)   7s.

JESUS! Name of wondrous love,
  Name all other names above!
Name at which must every knee
Bow in deep humility.

2 Jesus! Name of priceless worth
To the fallen sons of earth,
For the promise that it gave—
"Jesus shall His people save."

3 Jesus! Name of mercy mild,
Given to the holy Child,
When the cup of human woe
First He tasted here below.

4 Jesus! Only Name that's given
Under all the mighty heaven.
Whereby man, to sin enslaved,
Bursts his fetters, and is saved.

5 Jesus! Name of wondrous Love!
Human Name of Him above!
Pleading only this we flee.
Helpless, O Our God, to Thee.

46 (221)   C. M.

HOW sweet the Name of Jesus sounds
  In a believer's ear!
It soothes his sorrows, heals his wounds,
  And drives away his fear.

2 It makes the wounded spirit whole,
  And calms the troubled breast;
'Tis manna to the hungry soul,
  And to the weary rest.

3 Dear Name! the Rock on which I build,
  My Shield and Hiding-place;
My never-failing Treasury, filled
  With boundless stores of grace.

4 By Thee my prayers acceptance gain,
  Although with sin defiled:
Satan accuses me in vain,
  And I am owned a child.

5 Weak is the effort of my heart,
  And cold my warmest thought;
But, when I see Thee as Thou art,
  I'll praise Thee as I ought.

6 Till then, I would Thy love proclaim
  With every fleeting breath:
And may the music of Thy Name
  Refresh my soul in death.

47   8, 7. Iambic.

THERE is no Name so sweet on earth,
  No Name so sweet in heaven,—
The Name before His wondrous birth
  To Christ the Saviour given.
Chorus:—We love to sing around our King,
        And hail Him blessed Jesus;
      For there's no word ear ever heard
        So dear, so sweet as Jesus.

2 His human Name they did proclaim
  When Abram's son they sealed Him,—
The Name that still by God's good will,
  Deliverer revealed Him.
Chorus:—We love to sing around our King, etc.

3 And when He hung upon the tree,
  They wrote this Name above Him;

That all might see the reason we
  For evermore must love Him.
    Chorus :—We love to sing, etc.

4 So now, upon His Father's throne,
  Almighty to release us
From sin and pains, He gladly reigns,
  The Prince and Saviour Jesus.
    Chorus :—We love to sing, etc.

5 To Jesus every knee shall bow,
  And every tongue confess Him,
And we unite with saints in light,
  Our only Lord to bless Him.
    Chorus :—We love to sing, etc.

6 O Jesus, by that matchless Name,
  Thy grace shall fail us never ;
To-day as yesterday the same,
  Thou art the same for ever.
    Chorus :—Then let us sing around our King,
      The faithful, precious Jesus, etc.

EPIPHANY AND MISSIONS. .

48 (141)   7s.

SONS of men, behold from far,
  Hail the long-expected star !
Jacob's star that gilds the night,
Guides bewildered nature right.
Fear not hence that ill should flow,
Wars or pestilence below ;
Wars it bids and tumults cease,
Ushering in the Prince of Peace.

2 Mild He shines on all beneath,
  Piercing through the shade of death ;.
Scattering error's wide-spread night,
Kindling darkness into light.
Nations all, far off and near,
Haste to see your God appear !

Haste, for Him your hearts prepare,
Meet Him manifested there.

3 Here behold the Day-spring rise,
Pouring eyesight on your eyes:
God in His own light survey,
Shining to the perfect day.
Sing, ye morning stars, again!
God descends on earth to reign;
Deigns for man His life to employ:
Shout, ye sons of God, for joy.

49   11. 10.

BRIGHTEST and best of the sons of the morning,
Dawn on our darkness and lend us Thine aid;
Star of the East, the horizon adorning,
Guide where our infant Redeemer is laid.

2 Cold on His cradle the dew-drops are shining,
Low lies His head with the beasts of the stall:
Angels adore Him in slumber reclining,
Maker and Monarch and Saviour of all.

3 Say, shall we yield Him, in costly devotion,
Odors of Edom and offerings divine?
Gems of the mountain and pearls of the ocean,
Myrrh from the forest, or gold from the mine?

4 Vainly we offer each ample oblation,
Vainly with gifts would His favor secure;
Richer by far is the heart's adoration,
Dearer to God are the prayers of the poor.

5 Brightest and best of the sons of the morning,
Dawn on our darkness and lend us thine aid;
Star of the East, the horizon adorning,
Guide where our infant Redeemer is laid.

50   8. 7.

IN the vineyard of our Father,
Daily work we find to do;
Scattered gleanings we may gather,
Though we are but young and few;

Little clusters
Help to fill the garners, too.

2 Toiling early in the morning,
　Catching moments through the day,
Nothing small or lowly scorning,
　So along our path we stray;
　　Gathering gladly
　Free-will offerings by the way.

3 Not for selfish praise or glory,
　Not for objects nothing worth,
But to send the blessed story
　Of the Gospel o'er the earth,
　　Telling mortals
　Of our Lord and Saviour's birth.

4 Up and ever at our calling,
　Till in death our lips are dumb,
Or till—sin's dominion falling—
　Christ shall in His kingdom come;
　　And His children
　Reach their everlasting home.

5 Steadfast, then, in our endeavor,
　Heavenly Father, may we be;
And, for ever and for ever,
　We will give the praise to Thee;
　　Hallelujah!
　Singing all eternally.

51   8.8.8.6.

WE three kings of Orient are;
　　Bearing gifts, we traverse afar,
　Field and fountain, Moor and mountain,
Following yonder Star.
　　O Star of Wonder, Star of Night,
　Star with Royal Beauty bright,
　　　Westward leading, Still proceeding,
　Guide us to Thy perfect light.

2 Born a King on Bethlehem plain,
   Gold I bring to crown Him again;
      King for ever, Ceasing never
   Over us all to reign.
      O Star, etc.

3 *Frankincense* to offer have I,—
   Incense owns a Deity nigh:
      Prayer and praising All men raising,
   Worship Him, God on high.
      O Star, etc.

4 *Myrrh* is mine; its bitter perfume
   Breathes a life of gathering gloom;
      Sorrowing, sighing, Bleeding, dying,
   Sealed in the stone-cold tomb.
      O Star, etc.

5 Glorious now behold Him arise,
   King, and God, and Sacrifice;
      Heaven sings Hallelujah!
   Hallelujah, the earth replies.
      O Star, etc.

52 (122)   **7. 6.**

HAIL to the Lord's Anointed,
   Great David's greater Son!
Hail, in the time appointed,
   His reign on earth begun.
He comes to break oppression,
   To set the captive free;
To take away transgression,
   And rule in equity.

2 He comes with succor speedy
   To those who suffer wrong;
To help the poor and needy;
   And bid the weak be strong;
To give them songs for sighing;
   Their darkness turn to light,
Whose souls, condemned and dying,
   Were precious in His sight.

3 He shall come down like showers
  Upon the fruitful earth;
And love, joy, hope, like flowers,
  Spring in His path to birth.
Before Him, on the mountains,
  Shall peace, the herald, go;
And righteousness, in fountains,
  From hill to valley flow.

4 For Him shall prayer unceasing
  And daily vows ascend;
His kingdom still increasing,
  A kingdom without end.
The tide of time shall never
  His covenant remove;
His Name shall stand for ever;
  That Name to us is Love.

53 (301)   6. 4..

THOU, whose almighty word
  Chaos and darkness heard,
    And took their flight;
Hear us, we humbly pray;
And where the Gospel day
Sheds not its glorious ray,
    Let there be light!

2 Thou, who didst come to bring,
On Thy redeeming wing,
    Healing and sight,
Health to the sick in mind,
Sight to the inly blind,
O, now to all mankind
    Let there be light!

3 Spirit of truth and love,
Life-giving, holy Dove,
    Speed forth Thy flight;
Move on the waters' face,
Bearing the lamp of grace,
And in earth's darkest place
    Let there be light!

4 Holy and blessed Three,
Glorious Trinity,
  Wisdom, Love, Might!
Boundless as ocean's tide
Rolling iu fullest pride,
Through the earth, far and wide,
  Let there be light!

54 (140)   7s.

AS with gladness men of old
   Did the guiding star behold;
As with joy they hailed its light,
Leading onward, beaming bright;
So, most gracious Lord, may we
Evermore be led by Thee.

2 As with joyful steps they sped
To that lonely manger-bed,
There to bend the knee before
Him whom heaven and earth adore;
So may we with willing feet
Ever seek Thy mercy-seat.

3 As they offered gifts most rare
At that manger rude and bare;
So may we, with holy joy,
Pure, and free from sin's alloy,
All our costliest treasures bring,
Christ, to Thee, our heavenly King.

4 Holy Jesus! every day
Keep us in the narrow way;
And, when earthly things are past,
Bring our ransomed souls at last
Where they need no star to guide,
Where no clouds Thy glory hide.

5 In the heavenly country bright
Need they no created light:
Thou its Light, its Joy, its Crown,
Thou its Sun which goes not down;
There for ever may we sing
Hallelujahs to our King.

55 (298)   7s.

HASTEN, Lord, the glorious time.
  When, beneath Messiah's sway,
Every nation, every clime,
  Shall the gospel call obey.

2 Mightiest kings His power shall own,
  Heathen tribes His Name adore;
Satan and his host, o'erthrown,
  Bound in chains shall hurt no more.

3 Then shall war and tumults cease,
  Then be banished grief and pain;
Righteousness and joy and peace
  Undisturbed shall ever reign.

4 Bless we, then, our gracious Lord,
  Ever praise His glorious Name;
All His mighty acts record,
  All His wondrous Love proclaim.

56 (299)   8. 7.

SAVIOUR, sprinkle many nations,
  Fruitful let Thy sorrow be!
By Thy pains and consolations
  Draw the Gentiles unto Thee!
Of Thy Cross the wondrous story
  Be it to the nations told;
Let them see Thee in Thy glory,
  And Thy mercy manifold!

2 Far and wide, though all unknowing,
  Pants for Thee each mortal breast:
Human tears for Thee are flowing,
  Human hearts in Thee would rest.
Thirsting as for dews of even.
  As the new-mown grass for rain,
Thee they seek, as God of heaven,
  Thee as Man, for sinners slain.

3 Saviour! lo, the isles are waiting,
    Stretched the hand, and strained the sight,
For Thy Spirit new-creating,
    Love's pure flame, and Wisdom's light.
Give the Word, and of the preacher
    Speed the foot and touch the tongue,
Till on earth, by every creature,
    Glory to the Lamb be sung.

57 (297)   7. 6.

FROM Greenland's icy mountains,
    From India's coral strand;
Where Afric's sunny fountains
    Roll down their golden sand ;
From many an ancient river,
    From many a palmy plain,
They call us to deliver
    Their land from error's chain.

2 What though the spicy breezes
    Blow soft o'er Ceylon's isle ;
Though every prospect pleases,
    And only man is vile :
In vain with lavish kindness
    The gifts of God are strown :
The heathen in his blindness,
    Bows down to wood and stone.

3 Shall we, whose souls are lighted
    With wisdom from on high,
Shall we to men benighted
    The lamp of life deny?
Salvation, O salvation !
    The joyful sound proclaim,
Till each remotest nation
    Has learned Messiah's Name.

4 Waft, waft, ye winds, His story,
    And you, ye waters, roll,
Till, like a sea of glory,
    It spreads from pole to pole;

Till o'er our ransomed nature
The Lamb for sinners slain,
Redeemer, King, Creator,
In bliss return to reign.

THE PASSION.

5S (150) *   C. M.

THERE is a fountain filled with blood
    Drawn from Immanuel's veins ;
And sinners, plunged beneath that flood,
    Lose all their guilty stains.

2 The dying thief rejoiced to see
    That fountain in his day;
And there may I, as vile as he,
    Wash all my sins away!

3 Dear dying Lamb, Thy precious Blood
    Shall never lose its power,
Till all the ransomed Church of God
    Be saved, to sin no more.

4 Lord, I believe Thou hast prepared
    (Unworthy though I be)
For me a blood-bought free reward,
    A golden harp for me!

5 'T is strung and tuned for endless years,
    And formed by power divine
To sound in God the Father's ears
    No other name but Thine.

---

*Verses 4 and 5 in Ch. B. om.

59 (157)   8. 7.

IN the Cross of Christ I glory,
   Towering o'er the wrecks of time;
All the light of sacred story
Gathers round its head sublime.

2 When the woes of life o'ertake me,
   Hopes deceive, and fears annoy,
Never shall the Cross forsake me;
   Lo! it glows with peace and joy.

3 When the sun of bliss is beaming
   Light and love upon my way,
From the Cross the radiance streaming
   Adds new lustre to the day.

4 Bane and blessing, pain and pleasure,
   By the Cross are sanctified;
Peace is there that knows no measure,
   Joys that through all time abide.

60 (367)   7s.

ROCK of Ages, cleft for me,
   Let me hide myself in Thee!
Let the Water and the Blood,
From Thy riven side which flowed,
Be of sin the perfect cure,
Save me, Lord, and make me pure.

2 Not the labors of my hands
Can fulfill Thy Law's demands:
Could my zeal no respite know,
Could my tears for ever flow,
All for sin could not atone:
Thou must save, and Thou alone!

3 Nothing in my hand I bring,
Simply to Thy Cross I cling;
Naked, come to Thee for dress;
Helpless, look to Thee for grace;
Foul, I to the Fountain fly;
Wash me, Saviour, or I die!

4 While I draw this fleeting breath,
   When my eyelids close in death,
   When I soar to worlds unknown,
   See Thee on Thy judgment throne,
   Rock of Ages, cleft for me,
   Let me hide myself in Thee!

61 (231)   7s.

JESUS, Lover of my soul,
   Let me to Thy bosom fly,
While the nearer waters roll,
   While the tempest still is high!
Hide me, O my Saviour, hide,
   Till the storm of life is past;
Safe into the haven guide;
   O receive my soul at last!

2 Other refuge have I none;
   Hangs my helpless soul on Thee:
Leave, ah, leave me not alone,
   Still support and comfort me!
All my trust on Thee is stayed,
   All my help from Thee I bring:
Cover my defenceless head
   With the shadow of Thy wing.

3 Thou, O Christ, art all I want;
   More than all in Thee I find:
Raise the fallen, cheer the faint,
   Heal the sick and lead the blind.
Just and holy is Thy Name;
   I am all unrighteousness:
False and full of sin I am;
   Thou art full of truth and grace.

4 Plenteous grace with Thee is found,
   Grace to cover all my sin;
Let the healing streams abound;
   Make and keep me pure within.
Thou of life the Fountain art,
   Freely let me take of Thee:
Spring Thou up within my heart,
   Rise to all eternity.

62 (368)

I LAY my sins on Jesus,
  The spotless Lamb of God;
He bears them all, and frees us
From the accursed load.
I bring my guilt to Jesus,
  To wash my crimson stains
White, in His Blood so precious,
  Till not a spot remains.

2 I lay my wants on Jesus;
  All fulness dwells in Him;
He heals all my diseases,
  He doth my soul redeem.
I lay my griefs on Jesus,
  My burdens and my cares;
He from them all releases,
  He all my sorrows shares.

3 I long to be like Jesus,
  Meek, loving, lowly, mild;
I long to be like Jesus,
  The Father's holy child.
I long to be with Jesus,
  Amid the heavenly throng,
To sing with saints His praises,
  To learn the angels' song.

PALM SUNDAY.

63 (527)

WHEN, His salvation bringing,
  To Zion Jesus came,
The children all stood singing
  Hosanna to His Name.
Nor did their zeal offend Him,
  But, as He rode along,
He let them still attend Him,
  And smiled to hear their song.

2 And since the Lord retaineth
   His love for children still,
Though now as King He reigneth
   On Zion's heavenly hill:
We'll flock around His banner,
   Who sits upon the throne,
And cry aloud, Hosanna
   To David's royal Son.

3 For should we fail proclaiming
   Our great Redeemer's praise,
The stones, our silence shaming,
   Would their Hosannas raise.
But shall we only render
   The tribute of our words?
No: while our hearts are tender,
   They, too, shall be the Lord's.

64 (214)   *Gloria, laus, et honor.*   7. 6.

ALL glory, praise, and honor
   To Thee, Redeemer King:
To whom the lips of children
   Made sweet hosannas ring.

2 Thou art the King of Israel,
   Thou David's royal Son,
Who in the Lord's name comest,
   The King and Blessed One!

3 The company of angels
   Are praising Thee on high,
And mortal men, and all things
   Created, make reply.

4 The people of the Hebrews
   With palms before Thee went;
Our praise and prayer and anthems
   Before Thee we present.

F

5 To Thee before Thy Passion
   They sang their hymns of praise ;
To Thee, now high exalted,
   Our melody we raise.

6 Thou didst accept their praises;
   Accept the prayers we bring,
Who in all good delightest,
   Thou good and gracious King!

65 (167)   C. M.

O THOU who through this holy week
      Didst suffer for us all;
The sick to cure, the lost to seek,
   To raise up them that fall:

2 We cannot understand the woe
   Thy Love was pleased to bear:
O Lamb of God, we only know
   That all our hopes are there!

3 Thy feet the path of suffering trod ;
   Thy hand the victory won:
What shall we render to our God
   For all that He hath done?

4 To God the Father, God the Son,
   And God the Holy Ghost,
By men on earth be honor done,
   And by the heavenly host.

66 (168)   L. M.

RIDE on, ride on in majesty!
      In lowly pomp ride on to die!
O Christ, Thy triumphs now begin
O'er captive death and conquered sin.

2 Ride on, ride on in majesty!
   The angel armies of the sky
Look down with sad and wondering eyes,
To see the approaching Sacrifice.

3 Ride on, ride on in majesty!
Thy last and fiercest strife is nigh:
The Father on His sapphire throne
Expects His own anointed Son.

4 Ride on, ride on in majesty!
In lowly pomp ride on to die!
Bow Thy meek head to mortal pain,
Then take, O Lord, Thy power, and reign.

67 (170)   8. 7.

HAIL, Thou once despised Jesus!
Hail, Thou Galilean King!
Thou didst suffer to release us:
Thou didst free salvation bring.
Hail, Thou agonizing Saviour,
Bearer of our sin and shame!
By Thy merits we find favor;
Life is given through Thy Name.

2 Paschal Lamb, by God appointed,
All our sins on Thee were laid;
By almighty Love anointed,
Thou hast full Atonement made.
All Thy people are forgiven,
Through the virtue of Thy Blood:
Opened is the gate of heaven;
Peace is made 'twixt man and God.

3 Jesus, hail, enthroned in glory,
There for ever to abide!
All the heavenly hosts adore Thee,
Seated at Thy Father's side:
There for sinners Thou art pleading,
There Thou dost our place prepare,
Ever for us interceding,
Till in glory we appear.

4 Worship, honor, power and blessing,
Thou art worthy to receive:
Loudest praises, without ceasing,
Meet it is for us to give.

Help, ye bright angelic spirits,
  Bring your sweetest, noblest lays,
Help to sing our Saviour's merits,
  Help to chant Immanuel's praise.

HOLY WEEK.

68 (163)   *Viva, viva, Jesu.*   6. 5.

GLORY be to Jesus,
    Who, in bitter pains,
Poured for me the life-blood
From His sacred veins!

2 Grace and life eternal
    In that Blood I find;
Blest be His compassion,
    Infinitely kind!

3 Blest through endless ages
    Be the precious stream,
Which from endless torments
    Did the world redeem!

4 Abel's blood for vengeance
    Pleaded to the skies;
But the Blood of Jesus
    For our pardon cries!

5 Oft as earth exulting
    Wafts its praise on high,
Angel hosts rejoicing
    Make their glad reply.

6 Lift we then our voices,
    Swell the mighty flood;
Louder still, and louder,
    Praise the precious Blood!

69 (435)   6. 4.

MY faith looks up to Thee,
    Thou Lamb of Calvary,
Saviour divine;

Now hear me while I pray :
Take all my guilt away;
Oh, let me from this day
   Be wholly Thine.

2 May Thy rich grace impart
Strength to my fainting heart,
   My zeal inspire;
As Thou hast died for me,
Oh, may my love to Thee
Pure, warm, and changeless be,
   A living fire.

3 While life's dark maze I tread,
And griefs around me spread,
   Be Thou my Guide;
Bid darkness turn to day,
Wipe sorrow's tears away,
Nor let me ever stray
   From Thee aside.

4 When ends life's transient dream,
When death's cold sullen stream
   Shall o'er me roll;
Blest Saviour, then, in love,
Fear and distrust remove;
Oh, bear me safe above—
   A ransomed soul.

70 (172)   7s.

SAVIOUR, when in dust to Thee
   Low we bend the adoring knee;
When, repentant, to the skies
Scarce we lift our weeping eyes;
O, by all Thy pains and woe
Suffered once for man below,
Bending from Thy throne on high,
Hear our solemn Litany!

2 By Thy helpless infant years,
By Thy life of want and tears,
By Thy days of sore distress
In the savage wilderness;

By the dread mysterious hour
Of the insulting tempter's power;
Turn, O turn a favoring eye,
Hear our solemn Litany!

3 By Thine hour of dire despair,
By Thine agony of prayer;
By the cross, the nail, the thorn,
Piercing spear, and torturing scorn;
By the gloom that veiled the skies
O'er the dreadful sacrifice;
Listen to our humble cry,
Hear our solemn Litany!

4 By Thy deep expiring groan;
By the sad sepulchral stone;
By the vault whose dark abode
Held in vain the rising God;
O, from earth to heaven restored,
Mighty, reascended Lord,
Listen, listen to the cry
Of our solemn Litany!

71 (182)

STRICKEN, smitten, and afflicted,
See Him dying on the tree!
'Tis the Christ by man rejected;
Yes, my soul, 'tis He! 'tis He!

2 Mark the Sacrifice appointed!
See who bears the awful load;
'Tis the Word, the Lord's Anointed,
Son of man, and Son of God.

3 Here we have a firm foundation;
Here the refuge of the lost;
Christ's the Rock of our salvation:
His the Name of which we boast.

4 Lamb of God for sinners wounded!
Sacrifice to cancel guilt!
None shall ever be confounded
Who on Thee their hopes have built.

72 (181) C. M.

ALAS! and did my Saviour bleed,
   And did my Sovereign die?
Would He devote that sacred Head
   For such a worm as I?

2 Was it for crimes that I had done,
   He groaned upon the tree?
Amazing pity! grace unknown!
   And Love beyond degree!

3 Well might the sun in darkness hide,
   And shut his glories in,
When Christ the mighty Maker died
   For man the creature's sin!

4 Thus might I hide my blushing face,
   While His dear cross appears;
Dissolve my heart in thankfulness,
   And melt my eyes in tears.

5 But drops of grief can ne'er repay
   The debt of love I owe.
Here, Lord, I give myself away:
   'Tis all that I can do.

73 (176) *O Haupt voll Blut und Wunden.* 7. 6.

O SACRED Head, now wounded,
   With grief and shame weighed down,
Now scornfully surrounded
   With thorns, Thy only crown!
O sacred Head, what glory,
   What bliss, till now, was Thine!
Yet, though despised and gory,
   I joy to call Thee mine.

2 How art Thou pale with anguish,
   With sore abuse and scorn!
How does that visage languish,
   Which once was bright as morn!
What Thou, my Lord, hast suffered,
   Was all for sinners' gain;
Mine, mine was the transgression,
   But Thine the deadly pain.

3 Lo, here I fall, my Saviour!
  'Tis I deserve Thy place!
Look on me with Thy favor,
  Vouchsafe to me Thy grace.
Receive me, my Redeemer;
  My Shepherd, make me Thine!
Of every good the Fountain,
  Thou art the Spring of mine!

4 What language shall I borrow
  To thank Thee, dearest Friend,
For this Thy dying sorrow,
  Thy pity without end!
O make me Thine for ever,
  And should I fainting be,
Lord, let me never, never,
  Outlive my love to Thee.

5 Forbid that I should leave Thee;
  O Jesus, leave not me;
In faith may I receive Thee,
  When death shall set me free.
When strength and comfort languish,
  And I must hence depart,
Release me then from anguish
  By Thine own wounded heart.

74 (187)   C. M.

JESUS, Thy soul, for ever blest,
    Hath gone among the dead,
And to his peaceful place of rest,
  The dying thief hath led.

2 And all for us; that when, ere long,
  We shall resign our breath,
We may not fear to go among
  The unseen shades of death.

3 In death's dark vale I soon must be,
  But I will nothing fear;
Thy rod and staff will comfort me;
  Thou hast Thyself been there.

75 (185)   8. 7. 7.

ALL is o'er, the pain, the sorrow,
    Human taunts and Satan's spite;
Death shall be despoiled to-morrow
    Of the prey he grasps to-night;
Yet once more, to seal his doom,
Christ must sleep within the tomb.

2 Fierce and deadly was the anguish
    Which on yonder Cross He bore;
How did soul and body languish
    Till the toil of death was o'er!
But that toil, so fierce and dread,
Bruised and crushed the serpent's head.

3 Close and still the grave that holds Him,
    While in brief repose He lies:
Deep the slumber that enfolds Him,
    Veiled awhile from mortal eyes;
Slumber such as needs must be
After hard-won victory.

4 We this night with plaintive voicing
    Chant His requiem soft and low;
Loftier strains of loud rejoicing
    From to-morrow's harp shall flow:
Death and hell at length are slain,
Christ hath triumphed, Christ doth reign.

EASTER.

76 (193)   7. 6.

THE day of Resurrection!
    Earth, tell it out abroad!
The Passover of gladness,
    The Passover of God!
From death to life eternal,
    From earth unto the sky,
Our Christ hath brought us over,
    With hymns of victory.

2 Our hearts be pure from evil,
  That we may see aright
The Lord in rays eternal
  Of Resurrection light:
And listening to His accents,
  May hear, so calm and plain,
His own All hail!—and hearing,
  May raise the victor strain.

3 Now let the heavens be joyful!
  Let earth her song begin!
Let all the world keep triumph,
  And all that is therein:
In grateful exultation
  Their notes let all things blend,
For Christ the Lord hath risen,
  Our Joy that hath no end.

77 *Fruehmorgens, da die Sonn aufgeht.* L. M.

ERE yet the dawn hath filled the skies,
  Behold my Saviour Christ arise;
He chaseth from us sin and night,
And brings us joy and life and light.

2 He feeds me, comforts and defends,
And when I die, His angel sends
To bear me whither He is gone,
For of His own He loseth none.

3 Strong Champion! For this comfort, see
The whole world brings her thanks to Thee;
And once we too shall raise above
More sweet and loud the song we love.

78 (192)   7s.

CHRIST the Lord is risen to-day,
  Sons of men and angels say.
Raise your joys and triumphs high;
Sing, ye heavens, and earth reply.

2 Love's redeeming work is done,
Fought the fight, the battle won;
Lo! the Sun's eclipse is o'er;
Lo! He sets in blood no more.

3 Vain the stone, the watch, the seal;
Christ has burst the gates of hell!
Death in vain forbids His rise;
Christ hath opened Paradise. ·

4 Lives again our glorious King;
Where, O Death, is now Thy sting?
Dying once, He all doth save;
Where thy victory, O Grave?

5 Soar we now where Christ has led,
Following our exalted Head:
Made like Him, like Him we rise;
Ours the cross, the grave, the skies!

6 Hail, the Lord of earth and heaven!
Praise to Thee by both be given:
Thee we greet triumphant now;
Hail, the Resurrection Thou!

79   *Luke xxiv. 34.*   S. M.

"THE Lord is risen indeed!"
      And are the tidings true?
Yes; we beheld the Saviour bleed,
      And saw Him living too.

2 "The Lord is risen indeed:"
      Then Justice asks no more;
Mercy and Truth are now agreed,
      Who stood opposed before.

3 "The Lord is risen indeed:"
      Then is His work performed;
The captive surely now is freed.
      And Death, our foe, disarmed.

4 "The Lord is risen indeed!"
      Attending angels, hear;
Up to the courts of heaven, with speed,
      The joyful tidings bear.

5 Then take your golden lyres,
      And strike each cheerful chord;
Join all the bright celestial choirs
      To sing our risen Lord.

ASCENSION.

80 (205) *   C. M.

THE Head that once was crowned with thorns
  Is crowned with glory now;
A royal diadem adorns
  The mighty Victor's brow.

2 The highest place that heaven affords
  Is His by sovereign right:
The King of kings and Lord of lords,
  And heaven's eternal Light.

3 The joy of all who dwell above,
  The joy of all below,
To whom He manifests His love,
  And grants His Name to know.

4 To them the Cross, with all its shame,
  With all its grace, is given;
Their name an everlasting name,
  Their joy the joy of heaven.

5 The Cross He bore is life and health,
  Though shame and death to Him;
His people's hope, His people's wealth,
  Their everlasting theme.

81 (201)   *Hymnum canamus gloriæ.*   L. M.

A HYMN of glory let us sing;
  New hymns throughout the world shall ring;
By a new way none ever trod,
Christ mounteth to the throne of God.

2 May our affections thither tend,
And thither constantly ascend,
Where, seated on the Father's throne,
Thee reigning in the heavens we own!

3 Be Thou our present Joy, O Lord,
Who wilt be ever our Reward:
And as the countless ages flee,
May all our glory be in Thee!

_____

*Verse 5 in Ch. B. om.

82 (200) *   7s.

HAIL the day that sees Him rise,
  Glorious, to His native skies!
Christ, awhile to mortals given,
Reascends His native heaven.

2 Him though highest heaven receives,
Still He loves the earth He leaves;
Though returning to His throne,
Still He calls mankind His own.

3 See, He lifts His hands above!
See, He shows the prints of love!
Hark, His gracious lips bestow
Blessings on His Church below!

4 Still for us His Death He pleads;
Prevalent, He intercedes:
Near Himself prepares our place,
Harbinger of human race.

WHITSUNTIDE.

83 (252) *Komm, O Komm, du Geist des Lebens.* 8.7.7.

COME, O come, Thou quickening Spirit,
  Thou for ever art divine:
Let Thy power never fail me,
  Always fill this heart of mine;
Thus shall grace, and truth, and light
Dissipate the gloom of night.

2 Grant my mind and my affections
  Wisdom, counsel, purity;
That I may be ever seeking
  Naught but that which pleases Thee.
Let Thy knowledge spread and grow,
Working error's overthrow.

*Verses 2 and 6 in Ch. B. om.

3 Lead me to green pastures, lead me
  By the true and living way,
Shield me from each strong temptation
  That might draw my heart astray ;
And if e'er my feet should turn,
For each error let me mourn.

4 Holy Spirit, strong and mighty,
  Thou who makest all things new,
Make Thy work within me perfect,
  Help me by Thy Word so true,
Arm me with that Sword of Thine,
And the victory shall be mine.

84 (249) *O Heil'ger Geist, kehr' bei uns ein.*

O HOLY Spirit, enter in,
  Among these hearts Thy work begin,
Thy temple deign to make us ;
Sun of the soul, Thou Light Divine,
Around and in us brightly shine,
  To strength and gladness wake us.
Where Thou shinest, Life from heaven
    There is given.
    We before Thee
For that precious gift implore Thee.

2 Left to ourselves we shall but stray ;
O lead us on the narrow way,
  With wisest counsel guide us,
And give us steadfastness, that we
May henceforth truly follow Thee,
  Whatever woes betide us :
Heal Thou gently, Hearts now broken,
    Give some token
    Thou art near us,
Whom we trust to light and cheer us.

3 O mighty Rock ! O Source of Life,
Let Thy dear Word, 'mid doubt and strife,
  Be so within us burning,
That we be faithful unto death,

In Thy pure-love and holy faith,
From Thee true wisdom learning!
Lord, Thy graces, On us shower,
By Thy power
Christ confessing.
Let us win His grace and blessing.

4 O gentle dew, from heaven now fall
With power upon the hearts of all,
Thy tenderness instilling;
That heart to heart more closely bound,
Fruitful in kindly deeds be found,
The law of love fulfilling;
No wrath, no strife, Here shall grieve Thee,
We receive Thee,
Where Thou livest
Peace and love and joy Thou givest.

85 (253)   C. M.

COME, Holy Spirit, heavenly Dove,
With all Thy quickening powers;
Kindle a flame of sacred love
In these cold hearts of ours.

2 Look how we grovel here below,
Fond of these trifling toys;
Our souls, how heavily they go,
To reach eternal joys!

3 Dear Lord, and shall we ever live
At this poor, dying rate?
Our love so cold, so faint to Thee,
And Thine to us so great?

4 Come, Holy Spirit, heavenly Dove,
With all Thy quickening powers.
Come, shed abroad a Saviour's love,
And that shall kindle ours.

86 (257)   7s.

HOLY GHOST, with light divine,
Shine upon this heart of mine!
Chase the shades of night away,
Turn the darkness into day.

2 Let me see my Saviour's face,
Let me all His beauties trace;
Show those glorious truths to me,
Which are only known to Thee.

3 Holy Ghost, with power divine,
Cleanse this guilty heart of mine:
In Thy mercy pity me,
From sin's bondage set me free.

4 Holy Ghost, with joy divine,
Cheer this saddened heart of mine;
Yield a sacred, settled peace,
Let it grow and still increase.

5 Holy Spirit, all divine,
Dwell within this heart of mine;
Cast down every idol throne,
Reign supreme, and reign alone.

6 See, to Thee I yield my heart;
Shed Thy life through every part.
A pure temple I would be,
Wholly dedicate to Thee.

TRINITY.

87

8.7.

BLESSED Father! Great Creator!
Humbly at Thy feet we bend;
To Thy throne for all Thy favors,
Youthful praises now we send.
Blessed Father!
To our youthful songs attend.

2 Blessed Jesus! Great Redeemer!
Sadly by Thy Cross we stand;
On that Cross Thou diedst to bring us
To the joys of Thy right hand.
Blessed Jesus!
Bring us to Thy heavenly land.

3 Blessed Spirit! Great Consoler!
  Make our hearts Thy dwelling place;
Teach us, guide us, sanctify us,
  And console us all our days.
    Blessed Spirit!
  Ever cheer us with Thy grace.

4 Blessed Father, Son, and Spirit,
  Glorious Godhead, Three in One!
Guide us to the heaven of heavens,
  Through the merits of the Son.
    Guide and guard us,
  Till we see Him on the throne.

88 (259)   C. M.

HAIL! holy, holy, holy Lord,
    Whom One in Three we know;
By all Thy heavenly hosts adored,
  By all Thy Church below.

2 One undivided Trinity
    With triumph we proclaim;
Thy universe is full of Thee,
  And speaks Thy glorious Name.

3 Thee, holy Father, we confess:
    Thee, holy Son, adore;
And Thee, the Holy Ghost, we bless,
  And worship evermore.

4 Hail! holy, holy, holy Lord,
    Our heavenly song shall be;
Supreme, essential One, adored
  In co-eternal Three!

89 (262)   6. 4.

COME, Thou almighty King,
    Help us Thy Name to sing,
    Help us to praise!
Father all glorious,
O'er all victorious,
Come and reign over us,
    Ancient of days.

G

2 Jesus, our Lord, descend;
  From all our foes defend,
    Nor let us fall;
  Let Thine almighty aid
  Our sure defence be made;
  Our souls on Thee be stayed;
    Lord, hear our call!

3 Come, Thou incarnate Word,
  Gird on Thy mighty sword,
    Our prayer attend:
  Come, and Thy people bless,
  And give Thy word success;
  Spirit of holiness,
    On us descend.

4 Come, holy Comforter,
  Thy sacred witness bear
    In this glad hour:
  Thou who almighty art,
  Now rule in every heart,
  And ne'er from us depart,
    Spirit of power!

5 To the great One in Three
  Eternal praises be,
    Hence, evermore!
  His sovereign Majesty
  May we in glory see,
  And to eternity
    Love and adore.

THE REFORMATION AND THE CHURCH.

90 (270)   8. 7.

ZION stands with hills surrounded;
  Zion kept by power divine;
All her foes shall be confounded,
  Though the world in arms combine.
    Happy Zion,
What a favored lot is thine!

2 Every human tie may perish ;
    Friend to friend unfaithful prove ;
  Mothers cease their own to cherish:
    Heaven and earth at last remove:
        But no changes
    Can attend Jehovah's love.

3 In the furnace God may prove thee,
    Thence to bring thee forth more bright,
  But can never cease to love thee ;
    Thou art precious in His sight :
        God is with Thee,
    God, thine everlasting Light.

91   7. 6.

THE Church's one foundation
    Is Jesus Christ her Lord ;
  She is His new creation
    By water and the Word :
  From heaven He came and sought her
    To be His holy Bride,
  With His own blood He bought her,
    And for her life He died.

2 Elect from every nation,
    Yet one o'er all the earth,
  Her charter of salvation
    One Lord, one Faith, one Birth :
  One holy Name she blesses,
    Partakes one holy Food,
  And to one Hope she presses,
    With every grace endued.

3 Though with a scornful wonder
    Men see her sore opprest,
  By schisms rent asunder,
    By heresies distrest,
  Yet saints their watch are keeping,
    Their cry goes up, "How long?"
  And soon the night of weeping
    Shall be the morn of song.

4 Mid toil, and tribulation,
  And tumult of her war,
She waits the consummation
  Of peace for evermore;
Till with the vision glorious
  Her longing eyes are blest,
And the great Church victorious
  Shall be the Church at rest.

92 (274)   *Ein feste Burg ist unser Gott.*

A MIGHTY Fortress is our God,
  A trusty Shield and Weapon;
He helps us free from every need
That hath us now o'ertaken.
  The old bitter foe
  Means us deadly woe:
Deep guile and great might
Are his dread arms in fight,
On earth is not his equal.

2 With might of ours can naught be done,
  Soon were our loss effected;
But for us fights the Valiant One
  Whom God Himself elected.
  Ask ye, Who is this?
  Jesus Christ it is,
Of Sabaoth Lord,
And there's none other God,
He holds the field for ever.

4 Tho' devils all the world should fill,
  All watching to devour us,
We tremble not, we fear no ill,
  They cannot overpower us.
  This world's prince may still
  Scowl fierce as he will,
He can harm us none,
He's judged, the deed is done,
One little word o'erthrows him.

4 The Word they still shall let remain,
  And not a thank have for it,

He's by our side upon the plain,
With His good gifts and Spirit,
Take they then our life,
Goods, fame, child and wife;
When their worst is done,
They yet have nothing won,
The Kingdom ours remaineth.

93   C. M.

I LOVE the Church, the holy Church,
The Saviour's spotless Bride;
And O, I love her palaces,
Through all the world so wide.

2 I love the Church, the holy Church,
That o'er our life presides—
The birth, the bridal, and the grave,
And many an hour besides.

3 Be mine through life to live in her,
And when the Lord shall call,
To die in her, the Spouse of Christ,
The Mother of us all.

94 (266)   8. 7.

GLORIOUS things of thee are spoken,
Zion, City of our God;
He whose word cannot be broken,
Formed thee for His own abode.
On the Rock of Ages founded,
What can shake thy sure repose?
With salvation's walls surrounded,
Thou may'st smile at all thy foes.

2 See the streams of living waters,
Springing from eternal love,
Well supply thy sons and daughters,
And all fear of want remove.
Who can faint while such a river
Ever flows their thirst to assuage?
Grace, which, like the Lord, the Giver,
Never fails from age to age.

3 Saviour, if of Zion's city
   I, through grace, a member am,
Let the world deride or pity,
   I will glory in Thy Name.
Fading is the worldling's pleasure,
   All his boasted pomp and show;
Solid joys and lasting treasure
None but Zion's children know.

95   C. M.

MY Church! my Church! my dear old Church!
   My fathers' and my own!
On Prophets and Apostles built,
   And Christ the corner-stone!
All else beside, by storm or tide,
   May yet be overthrown;
But not my Church—my dear old Church—
   My fathers' and my own!

2 My Church! my Church! my dear old Church!
   My glory and my pride!
Firm in the Faith Immanuel taught,
   She holds no faith beside.
Upon this Rock, 'gainst every shock,
   Though gates of hell assail,
She stands secure, with promise sure,
   "They never shall prevail."

3 My Church! my Church! my dear old Church!
   I love her ancient name;
And God forbid, a child of hers
   Should ever do her shame!
Her mother-care, I'll ever share;
   Her child I am alone,
Till he who gave me to her arms
   Shall call me to His own.

4 My Church! my Church! my dear old Church!
   I've heard the tale of blood,
Of hearts that loved her to the death—
   The great, the wise, the good.

Our martyred sires defied the fires
  For Christ the crucified ;
The once delivered faith to keep.
  They burned, they bled, they died.

5 My Church! my Church! I love my Church,
  For she exalts my Lord!
She speaks, she breathes, she teaches not,
  But from His written Word.
And if her voice bids me rejoice,
  From all my sins released;
'Tis through the atoning sacrifice,
  And Jesus is the Priest.

6 My Church! my Church! I love my Church,
  For she doth lead me on
To Zion's Palace Beautiful,
  Where Christ my Lord hath gone.
From all below, she bids me go,
  To Him, the Life, the Way,
The Truth to guide my erring feet
  From darkness into day.

7 Then here, my Church! my dear old Church!
  Thy child would add a vow,
To that whose token once was signed
  Upon his infant brow:—
Assault who may, kiss and betray,
  Dishonor and disown,
MY CHURCH SHALL YET BE DEAR TO ME,
MY FATHERS' AND MY OWN!

THE WORD.

96 (309)   C. M.

HOW precious is the Book divine,
  By inspiration given!
Bright as a lamp its doctrines shine,
  To guide our souls to heaven.

2 It sweetly cheers our drooping hearts
  In this dark vale of tears;

Life, light, and joy it still imparts,
And quells our rising fears.

3 This Lamp, through all the tedious night
Of life, shall guide our way,
Till we behold the clearer light
Of an eternal day.

97 (311)   C. M.

A GLORY gilds the sacred page,
Majestic like the sun ;
It gives a light to every age,
It gives, but borrows none.

2 The Hand that gave it still supplies
His gracious light and heat.
His truths upon the nations rise ;
They rise, but never set.

3 Let everlasting thanks be Thine,
For such a bright display
As makes a world of darkness shine
With beams of heavenly day.

4 My soul rejoices to pursue
The steps of Him I love,
Till glory breaks upon my view
In brighter worlds above.

98 (312)   C. M.

HOW shall the young secure their hearts,
And guard their lives from sin ?
Thy Word the choicest rules imparts
To keep the conscience clean.

2 'Tis like the sun, a heavenly light,
That guides us all the day ;
And through the dangers of the night
A lamp to lead our way.

3 The starry heavens Thy rule obey,
The earth maintains her place ;
And these Thy servants, night and day,
Thy skill and power express.

4 But still Thy Law and Gospel, Lord,
  Have lessons more divine ;
Not earth stands firmer than Thy Word,
  Nor stars so nobly shine.

5 Thy Word is everlasting truth :
  How pure is every page!
That holy Book shall guide our youth,
  And well support our age.

99 (316) *Erhalt uns, Herr, bei Deinem Wort.* L. M.

LORD, keep us steadfast in Thy Word :
    Curb those who fain by craft or sword
Would wrest the kingdom from Thy Son,
And set at naught all He hath done.

2 Lord Jesus Christ, Thy power make known ;
  For Thou art Lord of lords alone :
Defend Thy Christendom, that we
May evermore sing praise to Thee.

3 O Comforter, of priceless worth, .
  Send peace and unity on earth,
Support us in our final strife,
And lead us out of death to life.

The Small Catechism.

100 *Herr Gott erhalt uns fuer und fuer.* L. M.

LORD God, preserve from age to age
    The pure instructions of that page
Drawn forth, for all the world of youth,
By Luther from the Word of Truth :

2 That we, in Thy *Commands* well taught,
  Deplore our sins, as we all ought ;
Believe in Thee and Christ, our Lord—
Led by the Spirit through Thy Word.

3 To Thee "*Our Father*" may we pray,
  Who all our wants can take away ;
May we, *baptized.* our call fulfill.
And, as Thy children, do Thy will.

4 If any fall, let them not lie,
But to *Confession* quickly fly;
With faith the *Sacrament* receive.
Amen! A blessed end, Lord, give.

101 *Ach bleib bei uns, Herr Jesu Christ.* L. M.

LORD Jesus Christ, with us abide,
For 'round us falls the eventide,
Nor let Thy Word, our glorious light,
For us be ever quenched in night.

2 In these dark days that yet remain,
May we Thy Sacraments maintain,
And keep Thy Word, still true and pure,
And steadfast in the faith endure.

BAPTISM.

102 (323) *Ich bin getauft auf Deinen Namen.* 8. 7.

FATHER, Son, and Holy Spirit,
I 'm baptized in Thy dear Name;
In the seed Thou dost inherit,
With the people Thou dost claim,
I am reckoned;
And for me the Saviour came.

2 Thou receivest me, O Father,
As a child and heir of Thine;
Jesus, Thou who diedst, yea, rather
Ever livest, Thou art mine.
Thou, O Spirit,
Art my Guide, my light divine.

3 I have pledged, and would not falter,
Truth, obedience, love to Thee;
I have vows upon Thine altar,
Ever Thine alone to be;
And for ever
Sin and all its lusts to flee.

4 Gracious God, all Thou hast spoken
In this covenant shall take place;

But if I, alas! have broken
These my vows, hide not Thy face;
And from falling
O restore me by Thy grace!

5 Lord, to Thee I now surrender
All I have, and all I am;
Make my heart more true and tender,
Glorify in me Thy Name.
Let obedience
To Thy will be all my aim.

6 Help me in this high endeavor,
Father, Son, and Holy Ghost!
Bind my heart to Thee for ever,
Till I join the heavenly host.
Living, dying,
Let me make in Thee my boast.

CONFIRMATION.

103 (322)   8. 7.

BLESSED Saviour, who hast taught me
I should live to Thee alone;
All these years Thy hand hath brought me,
Since I first was made Thine own.
At the Font my vows were spoken
By my parents in the Lord;
That my vows shall be unbroken,
At the Altar I record.

2 I would trust in Thy protecting,
Wholly rest upon Thine arm;
Follow wholly Thy directing,
O my only Guard from harm!
Meet me now with Thy salvation,
In Thy Church's ordered way;
Let me feel Thy Confirmation
In Thy truth and fear to-day:

3 So that might and firmness gaining,
Hope in danger, joy in grief,

Now and evermore remaining
    In the catholic belief,
Resting in my Saviour's merit,
    Strengthened with the Spirit's strength,
With Thy Church I may inherit
    All my Father's joy at length.

104 (324)   L. M.

O HAPPY day, that stays my choice
    On Thee, my Saviour and my God!
Well may this glowing heart rejoice,
And tell its raptures all abroad.

2 O happy bond, that seals my vows
    To Him who merits all my love!
Let cheerful anthems fill His house,
While to that sacred shrine I move.

3 'Tis done, the great transaction's done;
    I am my Lord's, and He is mine:
He drew me, and I followed on,
    Glad to obey the voice divine.

4 Now rest, my long-divided heart,
    Fixed on this blissful centre, rest;
With ashes who would grudge to part,
    When called on angels' bread to feast?

5 High heaven, that heard the solemn vow,
    That vow renewed shall daily hear;
Till in life's latest hour I bow,
    And bless in death a bond so dear.

105 (325)   C. M.

MY God, accept my heart this day,
    And make it always Thine,
That I from Thee no more may stray,
    No more from Thee decline.

2 Before the Cross of Him who died,
    Behold I prostrate fall;
Let every sin be crucified,
    Let Christ be all in all!

3 Anoint me with Thy heavenly grace,
　Adopt me for Thine own;
That I may see Thy glorious face,
　And worship at Thy throne!

4 May the dear Blood, once shed for me,
　My blest Atonement prove,
That I from first to last may be
　The purchase of Thy Love!

5 Let every thought, and work, and word,
　To Thee be ever given:
Then life shall be Thy service Lord,
　And death the gate of heaven!

106 (326)*   7s.

THINE for ever! God of love,
　Hear us from Thy throne above;
Thine for ever may we be,
Here and in eternity.

2 Thine for ever! Lord of Life,
Shield us through our earthly strife;
Thou, the Life, the Truth, the Way,
Guide us to the realms of day.

3 Thine for ever! O how blest
They who find in Thee their rest;
Saviour, Guardian, heavenly Friend,
O defend us to the end.

4 Thine for ever! Thou our Guide,
All our wants by Thee supplied,
All our sins by Thee forgiven,
Lead us, Lord, from earth to heaven.

PRAYER.

107 (29)   7s.

COME, my soul, thy suit prepare,
　Jesus loves to answer prayer:
He Himself has bid thee pray,
Therefore will not say thee nay.

*Verse 4 in Ch. B. om.

2 Thou art coming to a King;
Large petitions with thee bring;
For His grace and power are such,
None can ever ask too much.

3 With my burden I begin;
Lord, remove this load of sin!
Let Thy Blood, for sinners spilt,
Set my conscience free from guilt.

4 Lord, I come to Thee for rest!
Take possession of my breast;
There Thy blood-bought right maintain,
And without a rival reign.

5 While I am a pilgrim here,
Let Thy love my spirit cheer;
As my Guide, my Guard, my Friend,
Lead me to my journey's end.

6 Show me what I have to do,
Every hour my strength renew;
Let me live a life of faith,
Let me die Thy people's death.

108 (536)   6. 4.

NEARER, my God, to Thee,
Nearer to Thee!
E'en though it be a cross
That raiseth me;
Still all my song shall be,
Nearer, my God, to Thee,
Nearer to Thee!

.2 Though, like the wanderer,
The sun gone down,
Darkness be over me,
My rest a stone,
Yet in my dreams I'd be
Nearer, my God, to Thee,
Nearer to to Thee!

3 There let my way appear
Steps unto heaven;

All that Thou sendest me
In mercy given;
Angels to beckon me
Nearer, my God, to Thee,
Nearer to Thee!

4 Then with my waking thoughts
Bright with Thy praise,
Out of my stony griefs
Bethel I'll raise;
So by my woes to be
Nearer, my God, to Thee,
Nearer to Thee!

5 Or if on joyful wing
Cleaving the sky,
Sun, moon, and stars forgot,
Upwards I fly;
Still all my song shall be,
Nearer, my God, to Thee,
Nearer to Thee!

FAITH AND LIFE.

109 (84)   *Psalm 23.*   S. M.

THE Lord my Shepherd is,
I shall be well supplied:
Since He is mine, and I am His,
What can I want beside?

2 He leads me to the place
Where heavenly pasture grows,
Where living waters gently pass,
And full salvation flows.

3 If e'er I go astray,
He doth my soul reclaim,
And guides me in His own right way,
For His most holy Name.

4 While He affords His aid,
I cannot yield to fear:

Tho' I should walk thro' death's dark shade,
My Shepherd's with me there.

5 The bounties of Thy love
Shall crown my following days;
Nor from Thy house will I remove,
Nor cease to speak Thy praise.

110 (69)   C. M.

HOLY and reverend is the Name
Of our eternal King.
Thrice holy, Lord! the angels cry:
Thrice holy, let us sing.

2 Holy is He in all His works,
And saints are His delight;
But sinners and their wicked ways
Shall perish from His sight.

3 The deepest reverence of the mind
Pay, O my soul, to God;
Lift with thy hands a holy heart
To His sublime abode.

4 Thou, righteous God! preserve my soul
From all pollution free:
The pure in heart are Thy delight,
And they Thy face shall see.

111 (90)   C. M.

SHINE on our souls, eternal God!
With rays of beauty shine;
O let Thy favor crown our days,
And all their round be Thine.

2 Did we not raise our hands to Thee,
Our hands might toil in vain:
Small joy success itself could give,
If Thou Thy Love restrain.

3 With Thee let every week begin,
With Thee each day be spent,
For Thee each fleeting hour improved,
Since each by Thee is lent.

4 Thus cheer us through this toilsome road
  Till all our labors cease;
  And heaven refresh our weary souls
  With everlasting peace.

112 (366) *   L. M.

JUST as I am, without one plea,
  But that Thy Blood was shed for me,
And that Thou bidst me come to Thee,
O Lamb of God, I come, I come!

2 Just as I am, and waiting not
  To rid my soul of one dark blot,
  To Thee, whose Blood can cleanse each spot,
  O Lamb of God, I come, I come!

3 Just as I am, though tossed about
  With many a conflict, many a doubt,
  Fightings and fears within, without,
  O Lamb of God, I come, I come!

4 Just as I am, Thou wilt receive,
  Wilt welcome, pardon, cleanse, relieve,
  Because Thy promise I believe;
  O Lamb of God, I come, I come!

5 Just as I am; Thy Love unknown
  Has broken every barrier down;
  Now to be Thine, yea, Thine alone,
  O Lamb of God, I come, I come!

113 (377)   *Proverbs* 3 : 13, 17.   C. M.

HOW happy is the child who hears
  Instruction's warning voice,
And who celestial wisdom makes
  His early, only choice!

2 For she has treasures greater far
  Than east or west unfold;
  And her rewards more precious are
  Than all their stores of gold.

*Verse 4 in Ch. B. om.

H

3 She guides the young with innocence
  In pleasure's path to tread ;
A crown of glory she bestows
  Upon the hoary head.

4 According as her labors rise,
  So her rewards increase ;
Her ways are ways of pleasantness,
  And all her paths are peace.

114 (528)   7s.

JESUS, when a little Child,
    Taught us what we ought to be ;
Holy, harmless, undefiled,
  Was the Saviour's infancy ;
All the Father's glory shone
In the person of His Son.

2 As in age and strength He grew,
  Heavenly wisdom filled His breast ;
Crowds attentive round Him drew,
  Wondering at their infant Guest ;
Gazed upon His lovely face,
Saw Him full of truth and grace.

3 In His heavenly Father's house,
  Jesus spent His early days ;
There He paid His solemn vows,
  There proclaimed His Father's praise ;
Thus it was His lot to gain
Favor both with God and man.

4 Father, guide our steps aright
  In the way that Jesus trod ;
May it be our great delight
  To obey Thy will, O God !
Then to us shall soon be given
Endless bliss with Christ in heaven.

115 (106)*   C. M.

I HEARD the voice of Jesus say,
    Come unto me and rest ;

_____

*First part of each verse.

Lay down, thou weary one, lay down
Thy head upon my breast.

2 I heard the voice of Jesus say,
 Behold, I freely give
The living water; thirsty one,
 Stoop down, and drink, and live.

3 I heard the voice of Jesus say,
 I am this dark world's Light;
Look unto Me, thy morn shall rise,
 And all thy day be bright.

116 (378)   S. M.

WHAT cheering words are these!
 Their sweetness who can tell?
In time and to eternal days,
 "'T is with the righteous well."

2 In every state secure,
 Kept by Jehovah's eye,
'T is well with them while life endure,
 And well when called to die.

3 'T is well when joys arise :
 'T is well when sorrows flow:
'T is well when darkness veils the skies,
 And strong temptations blow.

4 'T is well when on the mount
 They feast on dying Love :
And 't is as well in God's account,
 When they the furnace prove.

5 'T is well when Jesus calls,
 "From earth and sin arise,
Join with the hosts of ransomed souls,
 Made to salvation wise."

117   H. M.

WHEN little Samuel woke,
 And heard his Maker's voice,
At every word He spoke,
 How much did he rejoice!
O, blessed, happy child! to find
The God of heaven so near and kind.

2 If God would speak to me,
    And say He was my Friend,
How happy I should be!
    O, how I would attend!
The smallest sin I then would fear,
If God Almighty were so near.

3 And does He never speak?
    O yes; for in His Word
He bids me come and seek
    The God that Samuel heard.
And every sin I well may fear,
Since God Almighty is so near.

4 Like Samuel let me say,
    Whene'er I read His Word,
"Speak, Lord, I would obey"
    The voice that Samuel heard;
And when I in Thy house appear,
"Speak, for Thy servant waits to hear."

118   *Advantages of Religion in Youth.*   C. M.

HAPPY is he whose early years
    Receive instruction well;
Who hates the sinner's path, and fears
    The road that leads to hell.

2 'Tis easier work if we begin
    To serve the Lord betimes;
While sinners who grow old sin
    Are hardened by their crimes.

3 It saves us from a thousand snares
    To mind Religion young;
With joy it crowns succeeding years,
    And makes our virtues strong.

4 To Thee, Almighty God, to Thee
    Our hearts we now resign:
'Twill please us to look back and see
    That our whole lives were Thine!

5 Let the sweet work of prayer and praise
Employ our daily breath:
Thus we're prepared for future days,
Or fit for early death.

119   *Eccles.* 12 : 1.   C. M.

REMEMBER thy Creator now,
In these thy youthful days:
He will accept thine earliest vow ;   .
He loves thine earliest praise.

2 Remember thy Creator now ;
Seek Him while He is near:
For evil days will come, when thou
Shalt find no comfort here.

3 Remember thy Creator now,
His willing servant be ;
Then when thy head in death shall bow
He will remember thee.

4 Almighty God, our hearts incline
Thy heavenly voice to hear ;
Let all our future days be Thine,
Devoted to Thy fear.

120   *Prayer for the Children of the Church.*   L. M.

DEAR Saviour, if these lambs should stray
From Thy secure enclosure's bound,
And, lured by worldly joys away,
Among the thoughtless crowd be found ;

2 Remember still that they are Thine,
That Thy dear sacred Name they bear ;
Think that the seal of Love divine,
The sign of cov'nant grace, they wear.

3 In all their erring, sinful years,
Oh let them ne'er forgotten be ;
Remember all the prayers and tears
Which made them consecrate to Thee.

4 And when these lips no more can pray,
These eyes can weep for them no more,
Turn Thou their feet from folly's way,
The wand'rers to Thy fold restore.

121   11.8.12.9.

I THINK, when I read that sweet story of old,
   When Jesus was here among men,
How He called little children as lambs to His fold,
   I should like to have been with them then.

2 I wish that His hands had been placed on my head,
   That His arm had been thrown around me,
And that I might have seen His kind look when He said,
   "Let the little ones come unto Me."

3 Yet still to His footstool in prayer I may go,
   And ask for a share in His love;
And if I thus earnestly seek Him below,
   I shall see Him and hear Him above;

4 In that beautiful place He has gone to prepare
   For all who are washed and forgiven;
Full many dear children are gathering there,
   "For of such is the kingdom of heaven."

5 But thousands and thousands who wander and fall,
   Never heard of that heavenly home:
I wish they could know there is room for them all,
   And that Jesus has bid them to come.

6 And O, how I long for that glorious time,
   The sweetest and brightest and best,
When the dear little children of every clime,
   Shall crowd to His arms and be blest.

122   7s.

JESUS, Saviour, Son of God,
   Who for me life's pathway trod,
Who for me became a child,
Make me humble, meek, and mild.

2 I Thy lamb would ever be;
Jesus, I would follow Thee;
And, like Samuel of old,
Always live within Thy fold.

3 Dearest Saviour, I am Thine,
Bid Thy Spirit on me shine;

Keep my weak and sinful heart,
Lest it should from Thee depart.

4 Teach me how to pray to Thee ;
Make me holy, heavenly :
Let me love what Thou dost love :
Let me live with Thee above.

123   7. 6s.

COME, let us sing of Jesus.
While hearts and accents blend ;
Come, let us sing of Jesus.
  The sinner's only friend :
His holy soul rejoices
  Amid the choirs above.
To hear our youthful voices
  Exulting in His love.

2 We love to sing of Jesus,
  Who wept our path along :
We love to sing of Jesus,
  The tempted and the strong :
None who besought His healing.
  He passed unheeded by :
And still retains His feeling
  For us above the sky.

3 We love to sing of Jesus,
  Who died our souls to save :
We love to sing of Jesus,
  Triumphant o'er the grave ;
And in our hour of danger,
  We'll trust His love alone,
Who once slept in a manger,
  And now sits on a throne.

4 Then let us sing of Jesus,
  While yet on earth we stay,
And hope to sing of Jesus
  Throughout eternal day.
For those who here confess Him.
  He will in heaven confess,
And faithful hearts that bless Him,
  He will for ever bless.

124 (530)   7s.

L AMB of God, I look to Thee ;
   Thou shalt my example be ;
Thou art gentle, meek, and mild,
Thou wast once a little child.

2 Fain I would be as Thou art;
Give me Thy obedient heart.
Thou art pitiful and kind:
Let me have Thy loving mind.

3 Loving Jesus, gentle Lamb,
In Thy gracious hands I am.
Make me, Saviour, what Thou art,
Live Thyself within my heart.

4 I shall then show forth Thy praise,
Serve Thee all my happy days:
Then the world shall always see
Christ, the holy Child, in me.

125   8. 7.

G RACIOUS Saviour, gentle Shepherd,
   Little ones are dear to Thee ;
Gathered with Thine arms and carried
In Thy bosom may we be.

2 Tender Shepherd, never leave us
From Thy fold to go astray;
By Thy look of love direct us,
That we walk the narrow way.

3 Cleanse our hearts from sin and folly,
In the stream Thy love supplied,—
Mingled stream of Blood and Water
Flowing from Thy wounded side.

4 Let Thy holy Word instruct us,
Fill our minds with heavenly light;
Let Thy love and grace constrain us
Ever to pursue the right.

5 Taught to lisp the holy praises,
  Which on earth Thy children sing,
Both with lips and hearts we render
  Thanks and praises to our King.

126   8. 7.

CHRISTIAN children must be holy,
  Serving God from day to day;
Never is the time too early
  For a Christian to obey.

2 Jesus taught us in His childhood:
  Only eight short days He saw,
Ere He suffered circumcision,
  And obeyed His Father's law.

3 He who is our great Example,
  Let no moment run to loss;
Not one precious hour He wasted,
  From the cradle to the cross.

4 Soon He sorrowed, soon He suffered,
  We must meek and gentle be;
Little pain and little trial,
  Ever bearing patiently.

5 Soon He showed a Son's obedience:
  We must early learn to do
Not our own will, but our Father's,
  And be found obedient too.

127 (379)   7s.

CHILDREN of the heavenly King,
  As ye journey, sweetly sing;
Sing your Saviour's worthy praise,
Glorious in His works and ways.

2 We are travelling home to God,
In the way the fathers trod;
They are happy now, and we
Soon their happiness shall see.

3 O ye banished seed, be glad!
Christ our advocate is made;
Us to save, our flesh assumes;
Brother to our souls becomes.

4 Sing, ye little flock and blest:
　You on Jesus' soul shall rest:
　There your seat is now prepared,
　There your kingdom and reward.

5 Fear not, brethren, joyful stand
　On the borders of your land;
　Jesus Christ, your Father's Son,
　Bids you undismayed go on.

6 Lord, obediently we go,
　Gladly leaving all below;
　Only Thou our Leader be,
　And we still will follow Thee.

128　　　　*Weil ich Jesu Schæflein bin.*　7.7.8.8.7.7.

I AM Jesus' little Lamb,
　　Therefore glad at heart I am;
Jesus loves me, Jesus knows me,
All that's good and fair He shows me,
Tends me every day the same,
Even calls me by my name.

2 Out and in I safely go,
　Want and hunger never know;
　Soft green pastures He discloseth,
　Where His happy flock reposeth;
　When I faint or thirsty be,
　To the brook He leadeth me.

3 Should not I be glad and gay?
　In this blessed fold all day;
　By this Holy Shepherd tended,
　Whose kind arms, when life is ended,
　Bear me to the world of light?
　Yes! oh yes, my lot is bright.

129　　　　　　　　　　　　　　　7. 5.

HOLY Jesus, be my light;
　　Shine upon my way;
Through this tempting, changing life,
　Lead me day by day.

2 As the wise men came of old,
   Travelling afar,
Guided to Thy cradle throne,
   By a wondrous star;

3 So be Thou my constant Guide,
   Lead me all the way,
Till I reach Thy home at last,
   Nevermore to stray.

130   8. 7.

SAVIOUR, like a shepherd lead us,
   Much we need Thy tenderest care;
In Thy pleasant pastures feed us,
For our use Thy folds prepare.
      Blessed Jesus, Blessed Jesus,
   Thou hast bought us, Thine we are.

2 Thou hast promised to receive us,
   Poor and sinful though we be;
Thou hast mercy to relieve us,
   Grace to cleanse, and power to free.
      Blessed Jesus,
   Let us early turn to Thee.

3 Early let us seek Thy favor,
   Early let us do Thy will;
Blessed Lord and only Saviour,
   With Thy love our bosoms fill.
      Blessed Jesus,
   Thou hast loved us, love us still.

131 (444)   8. 7.

JESUS, I my cross have taken,
   All to leave and follow Thee;
Destitute, despised, forsaken,
   Thou, from hence, my All shalt be.
Perish every fond ambition,
   All I 've sought, or hoped, or known;
Yet how rich is my condition!
   God and heaven are still my own.

2 Man may trouble and distress me,
  'T will but drive me to Thy breast;
Life with trials hard may press me,
  Heaven will bring me sweeter rest.
O, 't is not in grief to harm me,
  While Thy Love is left to me;
O, 't were not in joy to charm me,
  Were that joy unmixed with Thee.

3 Take, my soul, thy full salvation;
  Rise o'er sin, and fear, and care;
Joy to find in every station
  Something still to do or bear.
Think what Spirit dwells within thee;
  What a Father's smile is thine;
What a Saviour died to win thee:
  Child of heaven, shouldst thou repine?

4 Haste thee on from grace to glory,
  Armed by faith and winged by prayer;
Heaven's eternal day's before thee,
  God's own hand shall guide thee there.
Soon shall close thy earthly mission,
  Swift shall pass thy pilgrim days;
Hope shall change to glad fruition,
  Faith to sight, and prayer to praise.

132 (156)   7s

FEEBLE, helpless, how shall I
  Learn to live, and learn to die?
Who, O God, my guide shall be?
Who shall lead Thy child to Thee?

2 Blessed Father, gracious One,
  Thou hast sent Thy holy Son;
He will give the light I need,
He my trembling steps will lead.

3 Through this world, uncertain, dim,
  Let me ever lean on Him;
From His precepts wisdom draw,
Make His life my solemn law.

4 Thus in deed, and thought, and word,
Led by Jesus Christ the Lord,
In my meekness, thus shall I
Learn to live and learn to die.

133   6. 5.

Do no sinful action,
    Speak no angry word,
We belong to Jesus,
    Children of the Lord.

2 Christ is kind and gentle,
    Christ is pure and true,
And His own dear children
    Must be holy too.

3 There's a wicked spirit
    Watching round us still,
And he tries to tempt us
    To all harm and ill.

4 But we must not hear him,
    Nor his bidding do,
But resist the evil
    And the good pursue.

5 For we promised truly
    In our infant days,
To renounce him wholly
    And forsake his ways.

6 We are new-born Christians,
    We must learn to fight
With the bad within us,
    And to do the right.

7 Christ is our own Master,
    He is good and true,
And His little children
    Must be holy too.

8 Glory to the Father,
    Glory to the Son,
Glory to the Spirit,
    While the ages run.

134 C. M.

MUST Jesus bear the cross alone,
　And all the world go free?
No, there's a cross for every one,
　And there's a cross for me.

2 How happy are the saints above,
　Who once were sorrowing here!
But now they taste unmingled love,
　And joy without a tear.

3 The consecrated cross I'll bear,
　Till death shall set me free;
And then go home, my crown to wear,
　For there's a crown for me.

135 (532) 8. 7.

SAVIOUR, Who Thy flock art feeding
　With the shepherd's kindest care,
All the feeble gently leading,
　While the lambs Thy bosom share,

2 Now, these little ones receiving,
　Fold them in Thy gracious arm!
There, we know, Thy word believing,
　Only there secure from harm!

3 Never, from Thy pasture roving,
　Let them be the lion's prey;
Let Thy tenderness, so loving,
　Keep them all life's dang'rous way:

4 Then, within Thy fold eternal,
　Let them find a resting-place,
Feed in pastures ever vernal,
　Drink the rivers of Thy grace.

136 8. 7.

LORD, a little band and lowly,
　We are come to sing to Thee;
Thou art great, and high, and holy,
　O how holy should we be.

2 Fill our hearts with thoughts of Jesus,
And of heaven where he is gone:
And let nothing ever please us
He would grieve to look upon.
3 For we know the Lord of Glory
Always sees what children do,
And is writing now the story
Of our thoughts and actions too.
4' Let our sins be all forgiven,
Make us fear whate'er is wrong:
Lead us on our way to heaven,
There to sing a nobler song.

137 (462)*   S. M.

SOLDIERS of Christ, arise,
And put your armor on,
Strong in the strength which God supplies,
Through His eternal Son;—
2 Strong in the Lord of Hosts,
And in His might and power:
Who in the strength of Jesus trusts
Is more than conqueror.
3 Stand then in His great might,
With all His strength endued;
But take, to arm you for the fight,
The panoply of God.
4 From strength to strength go on,
Wrestle, and fight, and pray:
Tread all the powers of darkness down,
And win the well-fought day.

CHARITY HYMNS.
138 (477)   S. M.

WE give Thee but Thine own,
Whate'er the gift may be:
All that we have is Thine alone,
A trust, O Lord, from Thee.

*Verses 4 and 6 in Ch. B. om.

2 May we Thy bounties thus
    As stewards true receive,
And gladly, as Thou blessest us,
    To Thee our first-fruits give.

3 O hearts are bruised and dead,
    And homes are bare and cold,
And lambs, for whom the Shepherd bled,
    Are straying from the fold!

3 To comfort and to bless,
    To find a balm for woe,
To tend the lone and fatherless,
    Is angels' work below.

5 The captive to release,
    The lost to God to bring,
To teach the way of life and peace,—
    It is a Christ-like thing.

6 And we believe Thy Word,
    Though dim our faith may be;
Whate'er we do for Thine, O Lord,
    We do it unto Thee.

139 (386)   6. 4.

O THOU best Gift of Heaven!
    Thou who Thyself hast given,—
For Thou hast died!
This hast Thou done for me:
What have I done for Thee,
    Thou Crucified?

2 I long to serve Thee more :
Reveal an open door,
    Saviour, to me;
Then, counting all but loss,
I'll glory in Thy Cross,
    And follow Thee.

3 Do Thou but point the way,
    And give me strength to obey;
Thy will be mine:

Then can I think it joy
To suffer or to die,
    Since I am Thine.

———

MISCELLANEOUS.

140 (139)   *New Year.*   7s.

WHILE with ceaseless course the sun
    Hasted through the former year,
Many souls their race have run,
    Never more to meet us here;
Fixed in an eternal state,
    They have done with all below;
We a little longer wait,
    But how little, none can know.

2 As the winged arrow flies
    Speedily the mark to find:
As the lightning from the skies
    Darts and leaves no trace behind;
Swiftly thus our fleeting days
    Bear us down life's rapid stream;
Upward, Lord, our spirits raise,
    All below is but a dream.

3 Thanks for mercies past receive,
    Pardon of our sins renew;
Teach us henceforth how to live,
    With eternity in view.
Bless Thy Word to young and old,
    Fill us with a Saviour's love;
And when life's short tale is told,
    May we dwell with Thee above.

141 (137)   L. M.

GREAT God! we sing that mighty Hand,
    By which supported still we stand:
The opening year Thy mercy shows,
Let mercy crown it till it close.

I

2 By day, by night. at home, abroad,
Still we are guarded by our God;
By His incessant bounty fed,
By His unerring counsel led.

3 With grateful hearts the past we own :
The future all to us unknown,
We to Thy guardian care commit,
And, peaceful, leave before Thy feet.

4 In scenes exalted or deprest,
Be Thou our joy, and Thou our rest;
Thy goodness all our hopes shall raise,
Adored through all our changing days.

5 When death shall interrupt our songs,
And seal in silence mortal tongues;
Our Helper, God, in whom we trust,
In better worlds our soul shall boast.

142   *Harvest Home.*   7s

COME, ye thankful people, come,
Raise the song of harvest home!
All is safely gathered in,
Ere the winter storms begin;
God, our Maker, doth provide;
All our wants are well supplied;
Come to God's own temple, come;
Raise the song of harvest home!

2 What is earth but God's own field,
Fruit to His own praise to yield?
Wheat and tares together sown,
Unto joy or sorrow grown;
First the blade, and then the ear,
Then the full corn shall appear:
Lord of harvest, grant that we
Wholesome grain and pure may be!

3 E'en the Lord our God shall come,
And will take His harvest home;
From His field, in that great day,
All offences purge away;

Give His angels charge at last
In the fire the tares to cast,
And the fruitful wheat to store
In His garner evermore.

4 Even so. Lord, quickly come
To Thy final harvest home:
Gather Thou Thy people in,
Free from sorrow and from sin;
There for ever purified,
In Thy presence to abide:
Come, with all Thine angels, come,
Raise the glorious harvest home.

143 (493) *National.* 6. 4.

GOD bless our native land!
    Firm may she ever stand,
        Through storm and night;
When the wild tempests rave,
Ruler of wind and wave,
Do Thou our country save
        By Thy great might!

2 For her our prayer shall rise
To God above the skies;
        On Him we wait:
Thou who art ever nigh,
Guarding with watchful eye,
To Thee aloud we cry,
        God save the State!

THE LAST THINGS.

144 (542) 11s.

I WOULD not live alway; I ask not to stay
    Where storm after storm rises dark o'er the way:
The few lurid mornings that dawn on us here
Are enough for life's woes, full enough for its cheer.

2 I would not live alway, thus fettered by sin,
Temptation without, and corruption within:
E'en the rapture of pardon is mingled with fears,
And the cup of thanksgiving with penitent tears.

3 I would not live alway; no, welcome the tomb!
Since Jesus hath lain there, I dread not its gloom:
There sweet be my rest, till He bid me arise
To hail Him in triumph descending the skies.

4 Who, who would live alway, away from his God?
Away from yon heaven, that blissful abode,
Where the rivers of pleasure flow o'er the bright plains,
And the noontide of glory eternally reigns:

5 Where the saints of all ages in harmony meet,
Their Saviour and brethren transported to greet;
While the songs of salvation unceasingly roll,
And the smile of the Lord is the feast of the soul!

145   *The Happy Land.*   6. 4.

THERE is a happy land,
    Far, far away,
Where saints in glory stand,
    Bright, bright as day.
Oh, how they sweetly sing,
Worthy is the Saviour King,
Loud let His praises ring,
    Praise, praise for aye!

2 Come to that happy land,
    Come, come away:
Why will ye doubting stand,
    Why still delay?
Oh, we shall happy be,
When, from sin and sorrow free,
Lord, we shall live with Thee,
    Blest, blest for aye.

3 Bright, in that happy land,
    Beams every eye:
Kept by a Father's hand,
    Love cannot die.
Oh, then, to glory run,
Be a crown and kingdom won,
And, bright above the sun,
    We reign for aye.

146 8.6.8.6.C.

AROUND the throne of God in heaver,
 Thousands of children stand;
Children whose sins are all forgiven,
 A holy, happy band,
 Singing Glory, Glory, Glory be to God on high.

2 In flowing robes of spotless white,
 See every one arrayed;
Dwelling in everlasting light,
 And joys that never fade,
 Singing Glory, Glory, etc.

3 What brought them to that world above—
 That heaven so bright and fair,
Where all is peace and joy and love?
 How came those children there?
 Singing Glory, Glory, etc.

4 Because the Saviour shed His Blood
 To wash away their sin:
Bathed in that pure and precious flood,
 Behold them white and clean!
 Singing Glory, Glory, etc.

5 On earth they sought their Saviour's grace,
 On earth they loved His Name;
So now they see His blessed Face,
 And stand before the Lamb,
 Singing Glory, Glory, etc.

147 (579) C. M.

JERUSALEM, my happy home,
 Name ever dear to me!
When shall my labors have an end
 In joy, and peace, and thee?

2 When shall these eyes thy heaven-built walls
 And pearly gates behold?
Thy bulwarks with salvation strong,
 And streets of shining gold?

3 O when, thou city of my God,
 Shall I thy courts ascend,

Where evermore the angels sing,
Where Sabbaths have no end?

4 There happier bowers than Eden's bloom,
Nor sin nor sorrow know:
Blest seats! through rude and stormy scenes
I onward press to you.

5 Why should I shrink from pain and woe,
Or feel at death dismay?
I've Canaan's goodly land in view,
And realms of endless day.

6 Apostles, martyrs, prophets, there,
Around my Saviour stand:
And soon my friends in Christ below
Will join the glorious band.

7 Jerusalem, my happy home!
My soul still pants for thee;
Then shall my labors have an end,
When I thy joys shall see.

PROCESSIONAL HYMNS.

148 (447)   *Jesu, geh voran.*   5. 8.

JESUS, still lead on,
Till our Rest be won;
And although the way be cheerless,
We will follow, calm and fearless.
Guide us by Thy hand
To our Fatherland!

2 If the way be drear,
If the foe be near,
Let not faithless fears o'ertake us,
Let not faith and hope forsake us;
For through many a foe
To our home we go!

3 When we seek relief
From a long-felt grief;
When temptations come alluring,
Make us patient and enduring:

Show us that bright shore
Where we weep no more!

4 Jesus, still lead on,
Till our Rest be won:
Heavenly Leader, still direct us,
Still support, console, protect us,
Till we safely stand
In our Fatherland!

149   6. 5.

PRAISE the Lord of heaven,
  Praise Him in the height,
Praise Him, all ye angels,
  Praise Him, stars and light:
Praise Him, clouds and waters,
  Which above the skies,
When His word commanded,
  Did established rise.

2 Praise the Lord, ye fountains
  Of the deeps and seas,
Rocks, and hills, and mountains,
  Cedars, and all trees:
Praise Him, clouds and vapors,
  Snow and hail, and fire
Stormy wind, fulfilling
  Only His desire.

3 Praise Him, fowls and cattle,
  Princes and all kings:
Praise Him, men and maidens,
  All created things:
For the Name of God is
  Excellent alone,
Over earth His footstool,
  Over heaven His throne.

150 (587)   7. 6.

JERUSALEM the golden,
  With milk and honey blest,
Beneath thy contemplation
  Sink heart and voice opprest:

I know not, O I know not,
　What social joys are there!
What radiancy of glory,
　What light beyond compare!
2 And when I fain would sing them,
　My spirit fails and faints,
And vainly would it image
　The assembly of the saints.
They stand, those halls of Zion,
　Conjubilant with song,
And bright with many an angel,
　And all the martyr throng:
3 There is the Throne of David;
　And there, from care released,
The song of them that triumph,
　The shout of them that feast;
And they who, with their Leader,
　Have conquered in the fight,
For ever and for ever
　Are clad in robes of white!

DOXOLOGIES.

1　　　　　　　　　　　　　　　L. M.

PRAISE God, from whom all blessings flow;
　Praise Him, all creatures here below;
Praise Him above, ye heavenly host;
Praise Father, Son, and Holy Ghost.

2　　　　　　　　　　　　　　　C. M.

TO Father, Son, and Holy Ghost,
　The God whom we adore,
Be glory, as it was, is now,
　And shall be evermore.

3　　　　　　　　　　　　　　　S. M.

TO God the Father, Son,
　And Spirit, One in Three,
Be glory, as it was, is now,
　And shall for ever be.

7. 6.

TO Father, Son, and Spirit,
  Eternal One and Three,
As was, and is for ever,
  All praise and glory be.

6. 4.

TO God the Father, Son,
  And Spirit, Three in One,
  All praise be given:
Crown Him in every song;
To Him our hearts belong:
Let all His praise prolong
  On earth, in heaven.

7s.

HOLY Father, holy Son,
  Holy Spirit, Three in One
Glory, as of old, to Thee!
Now and evermore shall be.

7s.

PRAISE the Name of God most high:
  Praise Him, all below the sky;
Praise Him, all ye heavenly host,
Father, Son, and Holy Ghost:
As through countless ages past,
Evermore His praise shall last.

8. 7.

PRAISE the Father, earth and heaven,
  Praise the Son, the Spirit praise;
As it was, and is, be given
  Glory through eternal days.

8. 7.

PRAISE the God of all creation;
  Praise the Father's boundless love;
Praise the Lamb, our expiation,
  Priest and King, enthroned above;

Praise the Fountain of Salvation,
  Him by whom our spirits live;
Undivided adoration
  To the one Jehovah give.

10   **8. 7.**

GREAT Jehovah, we adore Thee,
    God the Father, God the Son,
God the Spirit, joined in glory
  On the same eternal throne:
    Endless praises
To Jehovah, Three in One.

11   **6. 5.**

FATHER, Son, and Spirit,
    Endless One in Three,
Now, henceforth, for ever,
  Glory be to Thee.

12   **11s.**

O FATHER, Almighty, to Thee be addrest,
    With Christ and the Spirit, one God ever blest,
All glory and worship from earth and from heaven;
As was, and is now, and shall ever be given.

Soli Deo Gloria.

INDEX OF FIRST LINES.